DEATH IS A LIAR

FINDING HOPE & HEALING WHEN YOU'VE LOST A LOVED ONE

DANIEL B LANCASTER

LIGHTKEEPER
BOOKS

FOR KARIS & JEREMIAH

IN MEMORY OF

HOLLI SUZANNE FISH LANCASTER

(August 6, 1963–March 29, 2016)

TABLE OF CONTENTS

PREFACE

My prayer is this book will strengthen your walk with God. May you draw closer to Jesus every day and be filled with the Spirit. May you sense deep in your spirit that God loves you and will never let you go.

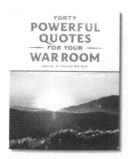  

I have included several bonus gifts that I believe will bless you. The free *Powerful Prayers Bonus Pak* which includes three resources to help you pray powerful prayers:

- 100 Promises Audio Version
- 40 Faith-Building Quotes
- 40 Powerful Prayers.

All are suitable for framing. To download your free *Powerful Prayers Bonus Pak* visit:

go.lightkeeperbooks.com/powerpak

I've also included an excerpt from my bestselling book Fear is a Liar. God has blessed many through this book and I wanted to give you a chance to "try before you buy." Order Fear is a Liar at go.lightkeeperbooks.com/e-fil

If you like the book, please leave a review. Your feedback will help other believers find this book easier and encourage me in my calling to write practical, powerful books to encourage, equip, and empower Christians throughout the world.

Every Blessing,

Daniel B Lancaster
Nashville, Tennessee — March 2022

PROLOGUE

This is a simple book about finding hope and healing after the death of a loved one. Ten months after we returned home from the mission field, I lost my wife of thirty years to ovarian cancer. No other experience in my life has shattered and shaped me more. If you have lost a loved one, I'm sure you can say the same is true.

In the months following Holli's passing, many friends told me I should author a book about Holli's death and how to grieve well. I smiled on the outside but shuddered on the inside thinking there was no way I could ever write about the torment I was experiencing. Even now, I feel humbled to author a book on grieving. There have been few times in the last five years I have thought I was "grieving well." *What does that even mean?*

About a year ago, though, I sensed the Spirit saying, "Write the book you wish someone had given you five years ago when you started your grief journey." You hold that book in your hands.

Grief comes in different shapes and sizes–there is no "one size fits all" approach. Grief looks different if you were married fifty years than if you were together for five years. Parents who lose a child don't grieve the same as a partner who loses a spouse. A twenty-one-year-old daughter who loses her mother grieves differently than a sixty-year-old son who loses his father.

Each grief journey is important and unique. So, comparing our grief stories does not help us heal, because only God knows every circumstance of our lives. God has a way of transforming our suffering into saving grace for others. That's what happened on the cross, and that's what is happening to those of us who grieve.

A thought about timing: If you lost a loved one recently, you might consider skipping the first two chapters. I describe the anguish I felt when Holli died, and it may be too much to process right now. Be kind to yourself. Trying to rush through the grieving journey will only drag it out longer. You don't need to push yourself to heal. Allow God's Spirit to carry you forward one step at a time.

If you are reading this book and have never lost someone close, you may think I am being melodramatic at times. I am not. I simply tried to describe my experiences as accurately as possible. If you think I'm being too emotional, simply keep reading. Learn as much as you can. One day, when you lose someone close, I believe you will have a different view. I hope you will pick up this book again and find comfort and support.

If you are grieving, I pray my vulnerability and transparency will help you know you are not alone. Through the years, I have attended many GriefShare® sessions and heard both widows and widowers share similar feelings and thoughts to the ones I describe in my journey.

Although each grief journey is different, everyone who grieves has similar problems and questions they must face to cross what David calls "the valley of the shadow of death" in Psalm 23.

My prayer is that reading my story will give you the faith you need to keep moving forward in your journey. May God fill you with hope as you read the testimony of a brother in Christ who floundered in sorrow but found a way to flourish after losing his soulmate. May you learn how to carry the memory of your loved one with you, and never leave him or her behind.

May God give us both His grace and peace as we start our journey together.

1

THE SHOCK OF DEATH

Jesus, my heart feels like a thousand knives are running through it. I am weary, spent, and just so sad. Please, help me! Hear my prayers. Hold me and my family up. Give us strength. Be present. Be persistent in your love. Carry us through this heartache. Sustain us. Bring us joy and hope.

- LISA APPELO

Holli was fifty-one years old when we discovered she had ovarian cancer. No one believed it. She had always eaten a healthy diet, exercised daily, and was rarely sick. I was the one who had suffered with a chronic illness for years. Everyone—including Holli—assumed I would be the first to die.

The five months following her diagnosis in October 2015 were filled with chemotherapy appointments, doctor visits, emergency ambulance trips, and watching my soulmate grow increasingly frail. When she was admitted to the hospital for a longer stay, I'd already used up my vacation time and could not be by her side during the day. For the last few months of her life, family members and friends volunteered to stay with Holli at the hospital for a week at a time. Every evening, I drove an hour-and-a-half between home and the hospital to see Holli as much as I could and give family members a break.

Everything seemed blurry, but we all kept pushing forward, one unsteady foot in front of the other. We were certain that God would heal Holli and kept praying for a miracle.

In March, we celebrated our daughter's birthday with lunch in Holli's hospital room. A few hours after everyone left, Holli suffered her first stroke. This did not take the doctors by surprise as blood clots to the brain are the way most women with ovarian cancer die.

After the stroke, Holli was dazed, but she could still talk. Just an hour later, she could no longer form words. We had to use a letter board so she could point to the letters and spell what she wanted to say. A mere two hours later, one of the most intelligent women I have ever known could no longer control her fingers to point to letters. Later that night, she could only talk with her eyes. I looked at the clock. It was 1 a.m., Easter Sunday morning.

Our family settled in at the hospital for the next three days. Holli's eyes lit up when we sang worship songs. Friends dropped by to pray with us, and emails and social media messages poured in from all over the world. The messages testified to the many people Holli affected in her life. She and I had often said, "You meet so many amazing people when you are a missionary." The truth is, *Holli was the amazing one.*

I can't remember much about those days other than life was surreal. What I do remember well, though, was the soul-crushing sadness mixed in with everything else. We cried so much; we grew numb. It seemed like we couldn't wake up from a bad dream, and time moved so slowly it felt like you could touch it.

Holli was called to her heavenly home the Tuesday morning after Easter. One moment she was in the room with us, and the next moment she was gone. The battle had traumatized us, but watching her die? It left us in shock. We couldn't think. We couldn't feel. We couldn't believe this tragedy had happened to our family. We felt like King David when he said:

> *I am worn out from my groaning. All night long I flood my bed with weeping and drench my couch with tears. My eyes grow weak with sorrow; they fail because of all my foes.*

> *Psalm 6:6-7 (NIV)*

Thankfully, three friends in Christ walked me through the first week of my grief journey. I never would have made it without them. They helped me buy the cemetery plots, make the funeral arrangements, and plan the service. They were Godsent, and I'm forever grateful to them.

A celebration of Holli's life was held on Friday. Each of our adult children memorialized their mother through a worship song, prayer, or testimony. By God's grace, I gave the eulogy—the hardest message I have ever preached. We had so many stories we wanted to share about this remarkable woman, but so little time. God's presence graced all who came to pay their respects to Holli Suzanne Fish Lancaster—wife, mother, daughter, sister, friend, and passionate follower of Jesus Christ, the Son of God.

The loving community at Union University (Jackson, Tennessee) surrounded us in the days after the funeral. Friends supported us with prayer and comforting conversations. Some brought food to the house, even for months afterwards. In many ways, we are here today because of them. For that, my family and I are grateful. We came to love each of them deeply.

Whispers

Most people don't know what to say when someone is grieving because they have never experienced grief themselves. Some try to comfort you by saying, "At least she is in a better place." When you are grieving, those words bring little solace. While it is true that your loved one is in the best place, you are in the worst place ever. How do you grapple with those soul-wrenching extremes? *It is hard to imagine heaven when you feel like you are in hell.*

Because many do not know what to say, they avoid talking to you altogether and may quickly excuse themselves when circumstances accidentally bring them and you together. Sometimes when you walk into a crowded room, people grow quiet and begin to whisper. I don't know why, but if I had to guess, I would say it may simply be human nature. What they don't realize is that whispers can make you feel even more alone in your grief.

Soon after Holli's death, a voice slithered into my suffering soul and began whispering lies to me. Satan claimed the shock of Holli's death would be a nightmare for the rest of my life. He made me believe the grief would follow me and, no matter whether I was awake or asleep, the grief would not stop. He hissed that my heart would never stop aching. He convinced me I wasn't going to make it through the pain. Satan smirked as he told me my tears and questions were evidence that my walk with God was too weak to weather this storm.

Satan seeks footholds in our lives during a tragedy because that is how he operates. He is evil and he has kept people in slavery to the fear of death for thousands of years (Hebrews 2:14-15). And trapped by that fear, we avoid talking about death because we are afraid it might rob us of a loved one, a partner, a child, a friendship—anything we hold dear.

Satan takes advantage of our pain, slithering up close to whisper lies. The enemy uses our most vulnerable time to launch an all-out assault on our faith. Armed with lies and confusion, he tries to convince us heaven is just a made-up story, and our loved one is gone … forever.

Even though Holli and I had been missionaries for years, I didn't have answers to the lies about death and heaven hurled my way. I was an easy target with little strength to fight back and no strategy to move forward. As a result, Satan knocked me down and kicked me every time I tried to get back up.

I grieve to think of all the believers through the ages who have suffered Satan's blows after losing someone dear. We need to stand against his attacks the moment they begin and understand that it is normal to struggle and feel helpless when we have lost someone dear to us. It is normal for people who are trying to reassure us to make comments that leave us feeling worse. And it is normal for us to feel shocked and have questions about heaven, hell, death, and God.

Questions

I remember the day Holli came home from the doctor's office with her diagnosis. We finally had an answer for the symptoms she had been experiencing. I ached with her when Holli told me the nurses at the cancer clinic looked at her with pity when she left her appointment. She and I talked about what Stage 4 ovarian cancer meant and how we would fight it. Then we prayed together and asked God to heal her. Afterwards, she turned to me and said, "We're going to beat this."

For the next five months, we stood on God's promises. We believed He would heal her. We bristled when a well-meaning doctor at the hospital asked me, "Hasn't anyone told you she's dying?" Not our Holli. Not now. She was going to live. We had a plan. We had God. We had confidence in our future.

But the God who holds the future had a different plan. And after God executed His plan and called Holli home, all I had was a bunch of questions, some of which included:

Why did God let her die? Holli loved God with all her heart. She was a faithful prayer warrior who interceded for others. She took her young family to the other side of the world to do mission work. Amid poverty and persecution in Southeast Asia, she ministered in the name of Jesus and guided many to the Kingdom of God.

Why did God let her suffer? People described Holli as "a sweet soul." A bit shy, her smile could flood a room with the presence of Jesus. She raised four children to love and follow God wholeheartedly. She brought beauty to this earth, but agonizing pain filled her last months. We watched our beautiful rose slowly wilt and fall to the ground.

Why did God take her when He did? Even now, it's hard to think of a worse time for Holli to have died. Our family had just returned from the mission field and was readjusting to life in America. Experts say it takes several years to adjust to living in your own country, especially if you have lived overseas for more than a decade as our family had. Our children faced major life transitions: high school graduation, college graduation, first-career decisions, and marriage. We had not even adjusted to her illness, and now we were having to try to accept her death.

I felt like Job in the Bible who said:

> *Moaning and groaning are my food and drink,*
> *and my worst fears have all come true.*
> *I have no peace or rest—only troubles and worries.*

> *Job 3:24-26 (CEV)*

What's the use of following God when He lets you down like this? I started asking this in my pain. *We tried to live a good life, but terrible events happened anyway. Nothing is safe. Everything can be destroyed in the blink of an eye.* Sometimes, I dared to wonder if choosing to follow Jesus had been a mistake.

The shock of Holli's death shoved my heart into a prison of anger. First came anger toward God. Then, I grew angry with those around me and withdrew from them. I felt like I had been sentenced to years in solitary confinement.

It didn't take long for my anger toward God and others to spiral into anger at myself. So much anger turned inward led to a depression that confined me like a straitjacket.

Finally, I opened my mouth like Job and began to curse the day of my birth (Job 3:1). To say I was in a dark place was an understatement.

Tears

Trauma causes flashbacks, and I couldn't stop replaying Holli's death. In the middle of a conversation, my mind would suddenly skip back to Holli's final days. I felt the agony again a million times—the moment she had the stroke and the questioning look in her eyes. I would remember the peaceful look on Holli's face as she slipped away, my daughter-in-law closing Holli's eyes for the last time.

Once a flashback ambushed me, it was incredibly difficult to live in the present. My emotions were all over the place—sometimes cold and frozen, then hot and boiling. Every time I ventured into public, I feared losing my composure. My heart cautioned, *If you start crying, you'll never stop.* It wasn't hard to believe the warning; my sorrow seemed like a bottomless pit.

Often, I struggled to do something as mundane as walking. It felt like half of me had died and everywhere I went, I labored to heave the "dead part" around. I felt like Satan had captured my soul, chained me to a wall, and was lashing the flesh off my back.

The memories were as hard as the flashbacks. Visions of life with Holli sapped all my strength. I would think back to our conversations on nightly walks and fight back tears the rest of the day. I would glance at a picture of her and feel like I might collapse, aching to see her sweet smile and hear her precious voice again. Memories of all we had done together—dating, our wedding, raising four kids, starting churches, going on family trips, and doing missionary work—overwhelmed me. I began suppressing every memory of Holli as I tried to fight the emotional battle within me.

The psalmist described his sorrow like this:

For I have eaten ashes like bread,
And mixed my drink with weeping
Because of Your indignation and Your wrath;
For You have lifted me up and thrown me away.

Psalm 102:9-10 (NASB)

Those words could be *my* words. Holli's Bible, her favorite books, her jewelry, and her clothes swirled like ashes around me. Losing her to cancer mixed everything with weeping—even my favorite meals seemed tasteless and dull. Exhausted by memories, I felt like God had picked me up and thrown me away.

Hearing a favorite song of ours or smelling her perfume in public made me shudder and my legs feel like heavy weights. I couldn't watch movies or television because most dramas have death or hospital scenes, and action movies are all about killing or being killed. I had never noticed this before but since Holli died, death was everywhere.

What had I done to deserve this? *Why had I been thrown onto this path with no choice?* Only one thing was certain: Rivers of tears were going to flood this journey and I wasn't ready.

Years

A few days after the memorial service, my friends returned to their normal routines—working, playing, and enjoying their families. They ate at restaurants and sat beside each other at church. They slept together at night and worked in the yard on Saturdays.

I did all those activities too, but I did them alone.

Even my closest friends didn't understand the intensity of my grief. They tried, but how could they? Unless you have lost a spouse, a child, or someone very close to you, there is no way to fathom how deeply death affects every part of your being.

Holli's death wrecked me, and my life shattered into a million pieces. On the outside, I looked fine. But everything had changed inside my heart and my mind. I was no longer the same person. I startled easily, and I often sighed involuntarily. I couldn't concentrate on anything for more than a few minutes at a time. Emotional ambushes waited behind every corner. Sleep was impossible. I slept beside oversized pillows at night to feel something—anything—while my heart suffocated in loneliness.

Death overshadowed every conversation, thought and activity. I woke up in the morning grieving, and grief walked beside me throughout the day. I went to sleep heartbroken and mourned all night in frightening dreams. Nothing made the grieving stop. Grieving had become my full-time occupation. And I was terrible at it.

Life before Holli died had moved forward sweetly and steadily. Sure, we had an occasional rough patch in the road, but they always smoothed out into the next season. But now? It was like an enemy had hurled grenades toward our family and destroyed everything. I had lost Holli. I had lost myself. Even more troubling, it felt like I had even lost God.

During those early weeks of grief, trusting God was difficult. I didn't want to read the Bible or pray. Singing worship songs was even harder as our family had led worship overseas many times, and every song filled my heart with special but painful memories. I sat at the back of the church on Sundays in case my heart couldn't take it anymore. Most Sundays, I left the service early.

Could I ever trust God again? He had taken away my best friend—forever. No other person had captured my heart as she did. So many people had believed God would heal her, yet He had chosen not to heal here on earth. I felt betrayed.

God's silence stunned me. After years of talking to Him and feeling close, His silence confused me. I wept and wondered why heaven remained still even as my soul writhed in misery. Like the psalmist, I begged God to speak and not be quiet:

> *To You I will cry, O Lord my Rock:*
> *Do not be silent to me,*
> *Lest, if You are silent to me,*
> *I become like those who go down to the pit.*

> *Psalm 28:1 (NKJV)*

I was in the pit and death was defeating me. Satan had blown out the candle on three decades of living, loving, and learning with the most incredible woman in the world. All that survived her death was me sitting in darkness. I felt abandoned and cursed—like a shrub in the wilderness with no water and no hope.

Thirty desperate days had passed since Holli died. My grief journey had only begun. I knew for certain that she was gone and not coming back, but everything else in my life was up for grabs.

The only thing I could ask myself-

How in the world am I going to do this?

2

THE STING OF DEATH

Jesus, I know you tell us you are close to the brokenhearted, but I don't feel you. I feel lost, hopeless, abandoned. My spirit is crushed, but I don't feel as if you are rescuing me. I need you. I need you to draw me close. I need you to lift my spirit, to rescue me. I need you to take my grief and give me a spirit of joy.

- DENA JOHNSON

Death destroys everything in its path. Like a monster tornado ripping through our community, stripping our beautiful home to a slab of bare concrete, Holli's passing left me feeling homeless—standing next to a pile of rubble. In a moment, everything was swept away like a butterfly in a 150-miles-an-hour wind. During the first year of mourning, I picked through the wreckage of my life trying to get back on my feet. And the sting of death was everywhere.

Overwhelmed

It's challenging to move forward when you believe God is hiding His face. Every place I walked, shadows and suffering peered back at me with cold-stone eyes, but it seemed like God was nowhere in sight. Like David, I found myself asking:

How long, O Lord? Will you utterly forget me?
How long will you hide your face from me?
How long shall I harbor sorrow in my soul,
grief in my heart day after day?
How long will my enemy triumph over me?

Psalm 13:2-3 (NIV)

The first year of my grief journey felt like our family was in a small sailboat in the middle of the ocean. What had started out as a pleasure trip had ended with a ferocious storm that took Holli's life and threw the rest of us overboard. Now we were in the water clinging to our little sailboat with a broken mast, torn sails, and no water to drink.

The ocean stretched as far as our eyes could see and we had no hope of rescue. The sun barely rose in the morning and happiness was a distant memory. Menacing thunderstorms filled each day, bringing more trouble and icy winds that made us shiver.

I wanted to feel confident again, but nothing I tried could shake the overwhelming grief. Holli's death had altered my default setting. My heart and mind had shifted to survival mode. Like the Psalmist, I cried out:

Save me, O God, for the waters have come up to my neck. I sink in the miry depths, where there is no foothold. I have come into the deep waters; the floods engulf me. I am worn out calling for help; my throat is parched. My eyes fail looking for my God.

Psalm 69:1-3 (NIV)

Deep waters surrounded me as I hung onto our capsized sailboat, but it felt like no one could hear my cry for help—not even God. Waves of sorrow battered my broken heart. Unlike the calming breakers on a seashore, these waves crashed into me with no warning. I never knew when they would appear, how strong they would be, or how long they would last. My days were filled with fighting one wave after another in a vast and unforgiving ocean.

I put a good face on to hide my grief, but secretly I was terrified a tsunami of sorrow might strike at any moment. A friend's careless comment here, or a co-worker's thoughtless criticism there, and I might be pulled under the breakers for the final time.

All of this and more were part of the sting of death.

Unprepared

Dark and gloomy thoughts flooded my mind that first year. Sometimes my chest ached so much from missing Holli that I thought I was having a heart attack. Other times I realized that I had been staring at a wall and couldn't remember anything about the previous half hour.

I was unprepared for the hardest spiritual battle of my life and began to ask questions like: *What if I'm grieving the wrong way? What if I'm doing something that will damage me emotionally for the rest of my life? Am I going crazy?*

Before Holli died, I had never walked through the valley of grief. Now, struggles and setbacks cluttered a path that

I had no clue how to navigate. I read books about grief, but they gave differing advice and added to my despair.

Some friends said I wasn't doing enough. Others said I was doing too much. All I wanted to do was ... nothing.

Grief erodes your self-confidence, so negative thoughts filled the splintered holes in my broken sailboat and threatened to sink it no matter what I tried. Thoughts like: *I'm not going to make it. I'm too needy. I'm too wounded. I'm too overwhelmed. I'm too lonely. I'm too _____ (fill-in-the-blank).*

All these thoughts gave birth to a dark idea I struggled to shake— *God had rejected me.* I wasn't sure what I had done and searched my memory for sin I had not confessed— anything that would explain what had happened. Like the Israelites in the Old Testament, I asked:

> *Will the Lord reject forever? And will He never be favorable again?*
>
> *Psalm 77:7 (NASB)*

My education and theology assured me that God had not left me, but my heart wasn't sure. My mind was a tangled mess, and I wasn't certain about anything anymore. Some will say I should have known better. I had attended the largest seminary in the world and received an excellent theological education. But in my four-year program, only one week was devoted to how to help others in their grief. As a result, I graduated knowing little about what healthy grief looks like.

I had preached and listened to countless sermons, but none gave answers for my current suffering and sadness. When is the last time *you* heard a sermon on grief? Our family had moved to Southeast Asia to share the good news that Jesus conquered death, but I would have failed the simplest test on helping someone grieve well.

Now that my soul wobbled with sorrow, I regretted not learning more about death and grief. Not just for me, but for other believers I had shepherded through the years. I thought of people I had known who had lost loved ones and how little I had understood their sorrow. If only I had known what to say and do. If only I had known how to help them walk through the valley of grief with hope.

On one difficult day, I asked myself, *What would Holli say about all of this if she were here?* I knew the answer. Holli would have encouraged me to look to God's Word. She would have quoted a verse like:

> *Your Word is a lamp to my feet And a light to my path.*
>
> *Psalm 119:105 (NKJV)*

I knew in my heart this was the right path. But thinking God had rejected me made opening His Word an agonizing experience. And reading even a sentence or paragraph of Scripture took much effort because of the heaviness of my grief.

All of this and more were part of the sting of death.

Afflicted

Death doesn't care if you have been a good person or a bad person in this life. All death wants is for you to die. Job experienced the sting of death even though he was a righteous man. In one day, he lost much of his wealth, most of his employees, and all his children (Job 1:13-19).

It's difficult to understand why God allowed Satan to torment Job. The Maker of everything good and holy stood aside and watched Satan afflict His servant Job. What's up with that?

Seeing the suffering that Job was experiencing, his friends asked questions like: *Why do bad things happen to good people? Why does God let evil prevail sometimes? Does God really care about us?*

None of these questions had good answers.

Holli's death devastated our family more than anything we had ever experienced. I lost my soulmate—the one who listened, cuddled, and sweetly corrected me when I needed it. Our grown children lost their mother—loyal defender, immovable anchor, and promise-keeper. We tried to comfort one another the best we could, sometimes with hugs or tears, and other times just sitting together quietly.

Holli's death blindsided me and left me crumpled in a heap, gasping for air. What would God take next? Would I experience financial ruin like Job? Would I lose my ministry? Would God take my children? Or like Job, would I lose my health?

> *Then Satan went out from the presence of the Lord and struck Job with severe boils from the sole of his foot to the top of his head. And Job took a piece of pottery to scrape himself while he was sitting in the ashes.*
>
> *Job 2:7-8 (NASB)*

Imagine boils from the top of your head to the soles of your feet—the sting of death leaves you a bleeding, oozing mess. It's hard to believe God cares for you while sitting on an ash heap scraping scabs off your body. God seems dark and distant. We feel like He doesn't care about us, and our sorrow makes our head feel twice as heavy as it is. Not sometimes. Most of the time.

All of this and more were part of the sting of death.

Perplexed

Doubt has been around a long time. Eve sinned in the garden because Satan tempted her to believe God couldn't be trusted. Satan whispered the same lies to me: God wasn't listening and didn't want to help. I knew in my mind this wasn't true, but the confusion was destroying my heart. Like ovarian cancer had taken Holli, doubt was taking me.

How could a missionary and pastor struggle with so much doubt? One truth I have learned is struggling with doubt is a normal part of the grieving journey. It is normal for death to affect your relationship with God. I don't want the evil one to convince you otherwise. That's why the Holy Spirit led Paul to write:

> *Brothers and sisters, we do not want you to be unin-formed about those who sleep in death, so that you do not grieve like the rest of mankind, who have no hope.*
> *I Thessalonians 4:13 (NIV)*

The Spirit knew Christians throughout the ages would struggle when other believers passed away. He also knew people rarely talk about death and that leads to many misunderstandings about the afterlife. Those misunder-standings result in errors that can cause Christians to grieve like the rest of humanity—as those with no hope.

Take heart; God is using your doubt in healing ways we will talk about later. Even in your doubt, God still holds you in the palm of His hand. He's never going to let you go.

Holli's passing exposed weaknesses in my faith that I didn't realize existed before she died. Being uninformed about death and holding wrong beliefs created cracks in the foundation of my faith. My heart needed to change if I were going to heal, but that's easier said than done. We can't just tell ourselves, "Don't doubt!" to stop all our questions. Life doesn't work that way. I know ... I wish it did, too. But it doesn't.

So, what do you do when faith and doubt occupy your heart at the same time? Thankfully, at some point in the early months of my grief, I began to hear the voice of God again. Even though it was difficult to pray and read God's Word at times, God gave me the grace of perseverance.

Sometimes my eyes were so blurred with tears that I couldn't see the words, but the Spirit helped me keep going. Other times everything was silent and dark when I prayed, but the Spirit helped me pray from the deepest parts of my soul.

I'm not sure exactly when it happened, but at the lowest point in my life, the Spirit of God gently reminded me of a story in Mark 9; A story about the struggle between faith and doubt.

Here's how I retell it:

> *After the transfiguration, Jesus walked down the mountain with Peter, James, and John. Approaching their camp, they noticed a large crowd had gathered and it looked like a riot might erupt.*

People were fervently arguing with one another. They were upset because Jesus' disciples hadn't cast a demon out of a boy. The demon was strong and had thrown the boy into many fires and tried to drown him several times. Exhausted from constantly caring for the child, his father had brought the boy to Jesus' camp and begged the disciples to perform an exorcism.

The disciples had tried to cast out the demon ... and failed. As Jesus approached, the boy fell to the ground convulsing and foaming at the mouth. Fear gripped the crowd and they stood frozen in silence.

Unaffected, Jesus asked the father what he wanted Him to do, and the man's response showed that he had lost all hope.

Tenderly, Jesus confronted his unbelief with the need for faith in God.

Convicted by Jesus' words, the father cried out, "I do believe; help my unbelief!"

Seeing his faith, Jesus cast out the demon. The boy was delivered, the crowd gave glory to God, and everyone left for their homes. Later that night, the disciples pondered all they had seen and heard that day while they ate their meal in reverent silence.

When the Spirit reminded me of this story, I knew I had lost all hope. I didn't believe Jesus could heal my broken spirit. And like the story, Jesus was challenging my unbelief. So, like the boy's father, I cried out to God from somewhere deep inside:

Lord, I believe. Help my unbelief!

What I didn't realize until later was I had just prayed a prayer that God always answers. Whenever doubts taunted me, I lifted those six simple but powerful words to heaven. I prayed those words every day for weeks.

Like a salve, the prayer began to soothe the sting of death. I prayed and prayed those six words, then prayed them some more. And after so many sad things had happened … finally … something good began to happen.

3

MY REDEEMER LIVETH

Jesus, you know what it is like to feel that God has abandoned you. You know pain and loss better than anyone else. Come to us now and let us feel your presence. We know that you are close to the brokenhearted and comfort those who mourn (Psalm 34:18). Help us to let you into our grief, to give you our anger and doubt. Jesus, pull us out of the void. In your name, Amen.

~ KATIE HARMON

Holli and I met in college during her first week on campus. Several months later, we were invited to the birthday party of a mutual friend and fell deeply in love—it was one of those "one enchanted evening" moments. I still remember walking her to her dormitory after the birthday party, skipping down the stairs after she went inside, and saying, "Thank you God for showing me the woman I'm going to marry."

Three years later, her dad officiated our wedding ceremony. Over 400 people were in attendance at the beautifully decorated church. The ceremony was perfect, from the exchanging of our vows to the music with harp and violin. I remember lifting my right hand in the air as she walked down the aisle in the same way I believe Jesus will greet His church when we join Him for eternity. Holli and I both cried through the whole ceremony, tears of joy and thanksgiving that God had brought us together.

It didn't take long after the wedding, though, for the honeymoon to wear off and for me to realize many places in my heart were damaged. The closeness of marriage has a way of revealing the rotting fruit left behind from growing up in an unhealthy home. I handled it the only way I knew how: I got busy.

I worked harder. I spent more time in worship. I prayed, studied the Bible, shared the gospel, authored books, served overseas. In short, over the span of thirty years, all my efforts centered on doing more and more good works for God.

Somewhere along the line, I switched from a heart-centered relationship with God to a mind-focused one. It was easier to figure out truth logically than deal with the chronic emotional pain inside. I knew many facts about God but only occasionally experienced Him as a caring, understanding Savior and Friend. The unresolved pain from my past squashed my ability to feel.

When Holli died, the pain from the past and the pain of losing her overwhelmed me. No amount of thinking and doing could suppress the pain.

God didn't create us to suppress our sorrow, but to express it to Him and others. He created us with the ability to heal from traumatic events. When we face the shock and sting of death, our brain chemistry changes. Our minds rewire themselves to make us slow down and deal with the pain instead of silencing it.

The changes in our brain as we grieve also cause us to lose focus. Thoughts swirl in our minds and time no longer passes in a steady state.

The Man of Sorrows

After Holli died, evenings were the hardest time of day for me. The nights stretched on and on into utter darkness and agonizing loneliness. You can only make so many phone calls, watch so many television shows, and read so many books until there is nothing left to do but be lonely. Sometimes it felt like all the darkness would put out the small light left in me.

One of these nights, trying to make the time pass, I was reading the book of Isaiah and discovered something about God I had never noticed before—His sorrow. Before Holli's death, I focused on what Jesus *did* during His ministry. After her passing, I focused on how He *felt*. Isaiah prophesied about Jesus this way:

> *He was despised and rejected by men, a man of sorrows and acquainted with grief.*
>
> *Isaiah 53:3 (ESV)*

Jesus *knows* sorrow and grief. This verse can easily become just another piece of information stored in our minds, but emotions are the currency of relationships. By sharing humanity's sorrow and grief, God is offering us the opportunity to experience Him at a deeper level.

When Holli died, the emotion portrayed in the Bible became more alive and real to me. I leaned in to learn more about the suffering and loneliness Jesus endured when He walked the earth. In the process, my heart toward God began to change.

For the first time, I *felt* what I believe Jesus may have felt when He cried over Jerusalem, and I cried over my family.

Just as Jesus wept when He saw His friends Mary and Martha grieving over the death of their brother, my heart broke in a new way for friends whose loved ones died untimely deaths.

Jesus withdrew in sorrow to a secluded place after He heard John the Baptist was beheaded. I similarly withdrew countless times after Holli passed away. The grief was so heavy that I needed time to sit in quietness, uninterrupted by human conversations. Like Jesus, I needed time to work through what had happened. And I needed space to come to terms with a world that was suddenly dark and unforgiving.

Unlike Jesus, though, the intensity of my grief shrouded God's presence like a thick fog that lasted a year. Slowly, as I took one step at a time to see God's sorrow, and as I kept repeating the prayer, "Lord, I believe. Help my unbelief," the fog began to lift.

The first image I saw was my Savior with tears running down His cheeks for me. Gazing at those tears changed me forever. Jesus was a *man of sorrows*. He understood exactly how I felt and knew the depth of my grief. Jesus knew the best path through the valley of grief. And I knew I could trust Him with my journey.

The God of Comfort

Not only did Jesus endure indescribable sorrow, but He also knows the great need for comfort. I do not believe anyone has needed more comfort than God the Father did when Jesus cried out from the cross, "My God, my God, why hast thou forsaken me?" (Matthew 27:46 NIV). Imagine how the Father felt gazing at the lifeless, cold body of His only Son in the tomb.

The Father accepted the sacrifice of Jesus for all people because it touched Him at the deepest part of His heart—the place where suffering, grief, and love meet. God suffered the gruesome death of Jesus because of His everlasting love for us and now He offers us the same comfort He gave Himself. The Bible says:

> The Father is a merciful God, who always gives us comfort. He comforts us when we are in trouble, so that we can share that same comfort with others in trouble.
>
> 2 Corinthians 1:3-4 (CEV)

One of the gifts of God's comfort is healing. And as my grief forced me to slow down and sit with God in new ways, I discovered He was not only healing my present grief, but also my past pain. And He was equipping me to comfort others in the future.

What the enemy had meant for evil, God was slowly turning to good.

The God Who Sends

Our Creator knows what we need. In His infinite wisdom and knowledge and goodness, He not only gives us comfort himself, but sends others to be a part of our healing.

One day, a friend who had walked a journey of grief told me about a Christian support group called GriefShare®. The GriefShare® program allows small groups of grieving people to meet each week to process their grief and support one another. My friend encouraged me to give it a chance.

To be honest, the thought of attending a support group scared me. *Am I ready to reveal my pain to perfect strangers? What if they ask me a question and I break down crying in front of everyone? What if I find out the way I am grieving is wrong? What if someone laughs when I share my broken heart?*

I got myself as far as the building where a group met, but the first night, I sat outside trying to convince myself to go in while replaying my objections in my mind. When I finally stepped inside, I was grateful to discover the group was a safe place filled with fellow strugglers. After we watched videos about grief featuring well-known Christian counselors, authors, and pastors, the leaders broke us into small groups where we all were free to share our sorrow. Every night I attended, I went home feeling stronger than I had felt when I walked in. Through those meetings, though my heart still hurt, the Spirit of God had sparked a glimmer of hope in me.

Grief is a fearsome foe that we cannot defeat by ourselves. Looking back on the first year of my journey, deciding to attend GriefShare® was one of the best decisions I made. If you are grieving right now, please consider gathering with others who are on the same journey. I pray you will experience God's grace together, and that doing so will make your burden of grief lighter.

The Way Forward

The journey of grief is not a straight line. Healing does not come instantly. You put one foot in front of the other and take time in the quiet to learn of God's own sorrow. You allow others to share your sorrow and healing comes one step at a time. Along the way, God offers His grace— even when we can't see or feel it.

When Holli died and the life I had known turned upside down, I felt like Bartimaeus, a blind beggar sitting in dusty ashes along the road outside Jericho. Mark tells us that when Jesus left Jericho, a crowd followed him. As he passed the beggar, Bartimaeus shouted, pleading for Jesus' attention (Mark 10:46-52). No matter how desperately he called out, the crowd kept moving, pushing Jesus further and further away.

As I read the passage anew, I saw myself on that dusty road. Like Bartimaeus, I desperately wanted Jesus to heal my broken heart and take away my pain. "Lord Jesus, Son of David, have mercy on me," I cried out until I was hoarse. It didn't seem as if He heard me, though. The crowd of fear, doubt, questions, and pain kept pushing Him away.

But then the procession stopped. In my mind's eye, I saw the disciples talking with Jesus and pointing at me. Jesus turned to His friends and said, "Call him." A few disciples approached and asked me to rise from my sackcloth and ashes. I slowly stood and made my way toward the King of Glory.

"What do you want Me to do for you?" Jesus asked me just as he did with Bartimaeus.

My voice quivered as I said, "Lord, I feel so hopelessly lost without Holli. I'm a broken man. I have no hope and feel so far away from you." My eyes welled up as I whispered, "Have mercy on me, Lord Jesus. I feel like I died when Holli died, and I want to live again. Please help me live again."

Jesus smiled and said, "Child, your faith has healed you."

I stumbled backward stunned. "But Lord," I said, "I have struggled with so much unbelief since she died. How could you ever forgive and heal me?"

Jesus' eyes sparkled when He said, "You only need the faith of a mustard seed, child. You have always had more faith than that in your heart."

Only a mustard seed? I thought. *How can that be?*

Jesus continued, "It's not the size of your faith, but the greatness of My Father's love that heals you."

With that word, the eyes of my heart were opened, and I could see with hope again. As I continued to spend time communing with Jesus, I could see how he had been carrying me all along like a shepherd carries a wayward lamb back to its fold. I had fallen over a towering cliff called *Holli's Death* and He had found me lying twisted and crumpled in the brambles below.

In my grief, I didn't see Jesus descend the cliff and pick up my bruised and bleeding soul. I was too delirious with pain to feel the healing ointment He put on my wounds and the bandages He applied to my broken limbs. Because of my desperate sobs, I did not hear Him singing soft songs of deliverance over me.

But now? Now I could see His great love. Hope rose in me like the sun on a beautiful spring morning. Jesus was healing the broken places in my heart.

▼ ▼ ▼ ▼ ▼

I am convinced that Holli saw Jesus heal me from her place in the great cloud of witnesses. Knowing her, she would have wanted to tell everyone what had happened. As I continued in prayer, God delighted me with a vision of Holli running to neighbors, saying, "Do I have a story to share with you about our great and mighty God!"

I saw a small crowd gather outside her heavenly mansion and listen to the details of how Jesus had healed another brokenhearted widower. One man raised his hands in worship saying, "Just like He did me. Just like He did me." I could see several of Holli's friends with tears of joy in their eyes.

Then, the story Holli shared of God healing me turned into a song of praise that rose higher and higher until it reached the throne of God. The song mingled with countless other songs throughout heaven. Those songs turned into a beautiful symphony of joyful adoration that lasted for hours.

As I turned my gaze back to Jesus in prayer, I saw Him smile.

Friend, Jesus wants to comfort and heal you, too. He sees your grief and knows your sorrow. He will use time with Him and others to restore your soul, if you will let Him. Let me show you a place to start.

4

THE GROW PLAN

Father, I offer this prayer to You to lift this
burden of grief from my heart. Shine your
eternal light onto my soul and let me feel the
joy of your love.
Guide me with Your wisdom, so I may under-
stand your plan. Let me lean upon Your
strength so I may grow strong once more
and emerge from my loss with a renewed
spirit of love and hope.
Amen.

- UNKNOWN

Grief is one of the toughest spiritual battles we face. Most of us have never experienced such intense emotions for an extended time, when everything feels abnormal and unpredictable. We've heard that denial is unhealthy, so we know we need to do and feel something. But the last thing we want is to get stuck in the nightmare we are living.

As days turn into weeks, and then into months, those of us suffering from sorrow start to wonder if our grief is ever going to end. *Am I going too slow? Have I missed something? Why is this taking so long?* At the same time, we're told we cannot rush grief. Nor can we "will" ourselves to get over it.

Our culture tells us that grief is something to check off the list—a problem to solve. The trouble is—grief never leaves the list if you cared deeply for the person who passed away. Grief is not a problem to be solved but a skill we learn. And few of us are prepared with the skillset grief demands.

As I walked through the valley of grief with Jesus, He directed me to focus on four concerns—goals, roadblocks, owning my brokenness, and walking it out with Him. In the beginning, I did not recognize what He was doing. But in time, I began calling this the GROW plan.

Each part of the plan will lead you to know Jesus more deeply, ground you in God's powerful truth, and renew your heart. In each step, you'll find a place to begin, no matter where you are in your grief journey. Moving forward one day, one step at a time, you'll find true north again. And as you progress in your journey, God will open doors, continually inviting you to come back and go deeper as you are ready.

In this chapter, I'll give a bird's-eye view of the plan. Then, I will share more details in the following chapters—one for each step of the plan. My prayer is that this simple plan will help you build the skills to navigate your grief journey as much as it has helped me.

Goals

The first step in the GROW plan is making new goals. The future we imagined and planned disappears when we lose someone close to us. In the beginning of our grief journey, the future is blank. You may not even know how to get through the next hour, let alone figure out the next five years.

Goals are the tool that helps us live out our faith in difficult times. At first, they are simply everyday actions to help us manage one day at a time. Our world has fallen apart, and simple daily goals help us get back on track when we have no idea which direction to turn.

Goals are nothing more than faith statements. Even when we are clueless about the future, we can make faith statements to keep us moving forward. By choosing to stand on the promises that God is with us, that He sends His comfort, and that He will see us through our journey, we start walking by faith again. Even the smallest goal is evidence that we still believe God is working in our lives.

When we are ready, Jesus leads us to make larger goals to replace earlier ones that have lost their meaning or no longer make sense. Death often exposes how many of our goals before we lost a loved one were based on earthly pursuits instead of everlasting ones. Jesus said:

> *What good is it for someone to gain the whole world, yet forfeit their soul?*
>
> *Mark 8:36 (NIV)*

Sadly, we often do not realize how much life we have lost until our spouse, or parent, or child dies. Instead of savoring time together, we constantly rushed from one activity to the next—much of it trivial. We would give it all back now to have one more conversation with our loved one while sipping coffee on the back porch.

After several months, Jesus gently began to expose the emptiness of several of my goals and encouraged me to focus my heart on pursuits that last—not on ones that pass. He reminded me:

> *But now faith, hope, and love remain, these three; but the greatest of these is love.*
>
> 1 Corinthians 13:13 (NIV)

Developing goals based on faith, hope, and love bring healing and a light for our path. These goals are based on eternity and honor our loved ones by energizing us to live again.

If making goals sounds overwhelming, don't be concerned. I am not talking about goal setting like you've heard all your life. I'm talking about faith statements that please God and keep us moving forward. God asks us to make small goals, not big ones, and I'll share an uncomplicated way to do this in the next chapter.

Roadblocks

The path through the valley of grief is full of roadblocks—obstacles like depression, loneliness, doubts, and suffering. Roadblocks slow us down and make the journey twice as long. Early on, I hit the roadblock of thinking life would always be bad and never get better. Jesus worked with me on that giant boulder for months.

When we grieve, Satan tries to alter the way we think about the future. The Bible says he is a murderer (John 8:44), a deceiver (Revelations 12:9), and an accuser (Revelation 12:10). Satan works at killing any hope we have about recovering from losing someone so important to us. He tries to convince us that God has deceived us about everlasting life. The enemy loves to accuse us of "not being enough" or "not having enough" whenever he gets the opportunity.

We are not powerless against Satan, though. Removing his roadblocks is the second skill of the GROW plan. The Bible shows us how to defeat Satan in our valley of tears:

> *And they have conquered him by the blood of the Lamb and by the word of their testimony, for they loved not their lives even unto death.*
>
> *Revelation 12:11 (ESV)*

We emerge victorious from our battle with Satan not because of anything we have done, but because of everything Jesus did! Jesus offered Himself as a sacrifice for our sins on the cross, and no roadblock on our journey can stand against the power of His blood. We can weather any hurricane from hell when we cling to the old, rugged cross.

We also overcome Satan by the word of our testimony— that's why attending a Christian support group like Grief-Share® is key to our healing journey. Testimonies are a powerful way to remove roadblocks from our path. When we hear other people's stories and how they are working through their grief, it builds our faith. Our own testimonies strengthen other believers as we praise God for small victories in our darkest moments. As we support one another, the evil one's schemes to block our journey forward shrink and finally wither away.

Learning how to overcome roadblocks is key in learning how to grieve.

Owning It

In the third step of the GROW plan, we focus on learning the skill of confessing our brokenness. Death destroys our defenses, stripping away all the ways we hide our faults or our pain. Our broken places rear their ugly heads—survival strategies like pride, anger, shame, and jealousy appear. Often, we are unaware of our brokenness until death shoves us on the path of sorrow.

We live in a broken world and develop survival strategies as children to deal with our pain. Some of us become people-pleasers while others comfort themselves by over-achieving. Some self-soothe by chasing perfection while others become control-freaks. We mask the suffering we feel as adults with these survival strategies; most of the time we don't even realize it.

The problem with survival strategies we developed in our childhood is that they do not work well for us as adults. That is why the third skill—Owning It—is important.

This skill teaches us to respond to God with surrender about our failed attempts to manage our life. We admit to God that we have been trying to solve our grief problems alone. We confess we have wandered away from Him and we do not know how to return.

God knows how much we struggle with pride and how difficult it is to admit our faults. As a result, our remorse touches His heart deeply. God declares:

> *I will bless those who have humble and contrite hearts, who tremble at my word.*

> *Isaiah 66:2 (NLT)*

The key to walking through the valley of grief is to find the path of blessing. Owning our brokenness gives us a humble and contrite heart that can confidently walk with Jesus through any circumstance. Repentance places us squarely on the path of God's favor.

Walking It Out

This journey through the valley of grief is not easy. There is no way to sugar coat it. No shortcut or detour around it. Oh, we can try to stuff it and avoid it, to distract ourselves with other things. But sooner or later we will come back to the realization that we are still on the path. The only choice is to go through it.

When Holli died, death lied to me and said she was gone forever. Death told me I would never stop hurting. Death said there was no resurrection. Fueled by my broken faith, Death sneered, "What's the use of living?" and crushed every ounce of hope in my soul.

God speaks a different language—the language of truth. He promises that Jesus is close to the brokenhearted, and that He is our Redeemer. He says:

> *I will guide you along the best pathway for your life.*
> *I will advise you and watch over you.*
>
> *Psalm 32:8 (NLT)*

God promises that He is with us on this journey. This does not mean we will not have doubt or frustration. Satan is the father of lies and will do anything to crush us. The enemy is crafty when it comes to trying to separate us from the God who loves us. In our vulnerability, Satan will constantly whisper lies. The only way to fight the lies is to know God's truth.

Jesus wants to help us through our grief. Satan wants us to get stuck in our grief. He'll rearrange the direction signs along the road, turning us left when we really need to go right. But we have more than a compass to help us find true north. We have more than a GPS. We have a guide who has gone before us, who knows the path, and who will walk with us every step of the way. We can be sure of our direction when we make God's Word our map.

▼ ▼ ▼ ▼ ▼

Jesus transformed my grief through the GROW plan, and I believe He will do the same for you. Let's take one skill at a time.

5

GOALS FOR THE JOURNEY

Dear Heavenly Father,
Thank you that you are a God who loves us
unconditionally. Thank you for being our Com-
forter in our deepest times of need. Lord I ask
that you would send hope and healing into my
heart right now. I'm hurting more than I ever
knew I could. I need you. I need your comfort
and strength. Help me take my next breath and
next step in you. Help me to know that it will
be okay because you are with me.
In Jesus' name, Amen.

- A.J. LUCK

The GROW plan begins with making new goals—
or faith statements, as I like to call them. You
might be wondering, "What's the use of having goals
when your life can change forever in a few seconds?"
Jesus understands how pain about the past makes us
skeptical of future efforts. He knows it is hard for us
to make goals when we are grieving. So even in our
darkest hour, Jesus has given us the Holy Spirit to
produce the fruit of faith deep within and give us the
ability to make faith statements in our sorrow.

Coming up with new goals for your new normal is an important part of the grief journey. When I realized I could overcome my sorrow by using small faith statements and simple actions to live these goals, it prevented me from slipping into the sloth marshes. Instead of wandering aimlessly in the land of no return, the goals God gave me guided me toward His powerful healing presence.

It is not the size of our goals nor the size of our faith that moves us forward, but the size of God's great love for you and for me. Jesus hears our cries for help when grief leaves us weak and breathless. That's why the first step we need to take is to start each day by asking the question ...

Lord, what are the 3 things you want me to do today?

The answer to this question is going to look different through different stages of your journey. This is not a cookie-cutter lesson on goal setting. It is a growth journey in learning to lean into Jesus and allow Him to direct you to step forward in faith, hope, and love, bringing healing and a light for your path.

While asking this short question may sound simple, learning to hear God's answer is a more challenging part of this skill set. There are many ways to listen for God's still small voice. One that I often use and share with others is listening through journaling.

When you've experienced trauma, your mind tends to race back and forth. Putting pen to paper and writing your prayer to Him is a powerful physical action that can help you slow down your racing mind and focus your attention on God.

As we talk about making faith statements, I want to show you what this listening can look like through my own letters with God. As we walk through the stages of making new goals, you'll see my honest and heartfelt questions to God. And you'll see Jesus' answers to me.

Listenting to and recording His responses turn our one-way communication into a conversation with our Savior. It quiets the noise around us for just a moment and gives us something to look back on when we need to see where we've been and how He's guiding us.

Just to be clear, these letters are not the inspired Word of God. Only the Bible holds that authority. When we listen for God's response, it must always line up with the truth of Scripture. That is why you will see many references to God's Word in His letters.

Whether you simply find clarity about what God's goals for you are or try journaling letters with Jesus yourself, I pray you will see how He walked with me through the valley of grief. And I hope my testimony will convince you that He will walk with you too. Let's start at the first step.

Russian Dolls

I've had a love-hate relationship with goals most of my life. Sometimes having goals has helped me succeed far more than I could have without them. Other times, they have felt like cruel taskmasters and choked the life out of me. When I lost Holli, goals seemed like the most absurd activity I had ever done.

My problem with goals was that I had been taught a goal had to be huge or I wasn't fulfilling all my potential. So, I struggled early in my grief journey when God gave me simple goals that anyone could do. In the journal entry below you will see how God showed me that any goal from Him, no matter how big or how small, is important in the Kingdom. Following His will is so much more important than what we do.

Dear Jesus,

Living without Holli is hard. Half the time I don't want to do anything but crawl in a hole somewhere and die. Last night at GriefShare®, we talked about moving forward and how it honors our loved ones. The lesson said setting goals is the first step, but I'm not sure how to do that anymore.

I've set and accomplished many goals throughout my life. I used to feel good about how productive I'd been. I sadly realize now that my goals often stole time from You, Holli, and the kids. Now that I've lost my soulmate, I don't want to repeat the same mistakes. What should I do?

Thanks for listening,

Your Child

▼ ▼ ▼ ▼ ▼

Precious Child,

I see how hard this is for you and hear your cries. Nothing is hidden from Me. Let's talk about making goals.

The first truth you should know about making goals is that you already make goals every day. A goal is simply the step you take to gain something you want. For example, you create goals when you make a checklist: clean the house, do the laundry, wash the dishes, and vacuum the floor. You want a clean house. A list of tasks (goals) assures you achieve your desire.

Like a Russian doll, goals nest within one another and go from small to large. The problem isn't making goals; it's knowing how big your goals should be.

This is what I want you to do: Ask Me each morning what My goals are for you that day. I will give you the best goals for each step of your grief journey.

Most of your life, you have made goals and asked Me to bless them. Now is the time to surrender control and let Me bless you by giving you goals that achieve everlasting results.

Love is My goal,

Jesus

The good news is God is Jehovah Jireh—our provider. In the same way He gave the Israelites just the right amount of manna in the wilderness each day, He will give you the goals you need every morning. We add so much pressure and heartache to our grief journey when we hold unrealistic expectations in our hearts about what we can accomplish.

Making it through the valley of grief is not a straight line to something more or bigger. God will show you what is right for today. God may give you a small goal today and a bigger one tomorrow. But it is just as likely He will give you a big one today and a smaller one tomorrow. We are such complex people living in a shattered world. God is the only one with the wisdom to know what is needed at each point in our journey.

Live It Out: Each morning, ask God what His goals are for you today.

One Day at a Time

One lesson I learned in my grief journey is the power of being present. So much of our world today is geared toward the future: getting married, getting a better job, saving for retirement. It's easy to live that way until you lose your soulmate. The future dissolves into smoke and all that is left are memories and the misery of today.

In the next journal entry, you will see how God gave me hope and comfort that He is in the day-to-day, even when life is hard. I discovered the only way to experience His presence was to be in the moment. As I practiced this skill repeatedly, I noticed my walk with Jesus moved from my head (which focuses on yesterday and tomorrow) to my heart (which is focused on today).

Dear Jesus,

Busted! I have made my own plans and have asked You to bless them too many times. I want to surrender and start walking by the goals You give me each day.

Here I am, Lord. Send me. What goals do You have for me today?

Thanks for understanding how hard this is,

Your Child

▼ ▼ ▼ ▼ ▼

Precious Child,

Your heart to surrender your goals reminds Me of what I did on the cross for you. Let's talk about your goal for today.

For most of your grief journey, I will give you several goals each day. But today, I'm only going to give you one: Take one day at a time. This goal is so important that you will hear Me say it every day of your journey.

Each day has enough trouble of its own. Mulling over your past or worrying about the future is a load no one can carry. Only the Father, Spirit, and I can live in the past, present, and future in a healthy way. I want you to be fully present today.

Every day with Me is the best day possible. You will find the strength you need when you follow Me one day at a time.

I'm with you always,

Jesus

Friend, I don't want you to think that living one day at a time was easy for me. The Lord consistently had to remind me that He was looking for progress and not perfection. The truth is that sometimes I went days without living one day at a time. Sometimes I went days without asking Jesus what the three goals He had for me that day were.

But this did not surprise Him. He would take me where I was and encourage me to start again. Most of the time I found I had skipped days not because the goals God had given me were too difficult, but because I had added to what He said, failed, and struggled to start again. Always remember that our Father's greatest joy is to see us win, not to shame us when we stumble.

Live It Out: Take one day at a time—start with today.

God's Goals

Working through our grief seems impossible at times, but it helps us to remember that God is using the bad that has happened to us to do something good. He has a plan for our lives even when everything has gone terribly wrong. The journal entries below gave me hope as I began to see the larger picture of God's plan and His feelings toward Holli before she was ever born.

Dear Jesus,

It's tougher to stay in the present than I thought. Help! It's easier for memories of past events or fears of the future to keep me frozen.

When I succeed in being present, tears and unanswered questions dominate that space. My gut reaction is to switch to the past or future to medicate the piercing pain.

I don't want to be like a five-year-old child who asks "Why?" repeatedly. But why? Why did You take Holli? How could her death be part of Your plan?

Still wondering,

Your Child

▼ ▼ ▼ ▼ ▼

My precious child,

Living one day at a time is challenging and you are making solid progress. Being hard on yourself won't shorten the journey.

Many believers measure spiritual maturity by how many verses they have memorized, or how long they have prayed, or the number of people they have led to Me. While good, these efforts aren't the mark of spiritual maturity. Your ability to stay in the present with Me is the true measure.

People ask the why question most often after someone dies. It's hard to understand when you view everything from earth. Seeing events from the Father's, Spirit's, and My perspective from heaven answers the question of "why."

The Father, Spirit, and I have enjoyed eternal life and indescribable love forever. Love passionately looks to expand, so We decided to create everything you see now to share Our love. Long before the universe was created, though, We knew that hate would try to kill love.

I committed to dying for humanity so love would win. That's why the Bible says I was "slain before the foundation of the world." That's also why the Father and Spirit seek to glorify Me at every turn. There is no greater way to reveal how much I love you than by dying in your place. I demonstrated infinite love by giving My life for every person who would ever live on earth.

To destroy hate, We set a plan in motion to redeem people and usher in a new heaven and earth. Think about that ... for millions of days, We have worked toward that goal. You have discovered that each hour of each day is unique. Imagine the complexity of a plan that takes every minute for every person into account. Then imagine the plan carried out with no mistakes.

The short answer to your "why" is that I have always loved Holli more than you can know. She was on my mind as I hung on the cross. The day she died was the best day for her to leave the earth and enter heaven. If you could see her now, you would be filled with overwhelming joy at the endless love she is experiencing.

Seeing her would fill you with boundless joy and expectation for the day you will join her in heaven. Celebration would replace your sorrow with never-ending praise to the Lamb Who is Worthy.

The sting of death has made it hard to trust anything in your life. You feel like a blind person shoved off your normal route by a shameless troublemaker. Nothing sounds or feels the same and you have lost your way. Even worse, the troublemaker's companions are shouting "Go this way!" or "Go that way!" to make you trip and fall in shame.

You must decide who you will trust to guide you back to the right path. Lean on me and not your own understanding. I am the Way, and you can trust me to lead you to the Promised Land.

I've never stopped holding your hand,

Jesus

Changing the way we think after losing a loved one takes time. It feels like we are in the spin cycle of a washing machine, and it never stops. Just when you think you've made progress, a picture, a song, or something else starts the cycle again.

The most helpful way I have found to stop the cycle is meditating on how it is for Holli in heaven. For many of us, we fall into the trap of thinking that human beings will someday have solved all the problems of this world. We believe that everything will be resolved by our efforts. But that is simply not true. Heaven is the only place where everything will be put right and restored.

Focusing on God's plans prevents the huge disappointments that can occur when we obsess on our own goals. Thinking through what our loved one experiences every day in heaven strengthens our hope. One of the keys to overcoming grief is starting small - and focusing on God's goals is no exception. Don't try to "see" the whole picture all at once but ask the Spirit of God to reveal it to you piece by piece every day. That's how strong friendships are built, and God has been all about connecting with us before time even began.

Live It Out: There is no greater love than that of Jesus. Choose to trust His love to lead you on the right path today.

Everlasting Goals

I am sure it does not feel like it now, but the day will come when you are thankful for how God has transformed your life through grief. You will review the past and praise God for deepening your relationship with Him and with others. You may have been a believer for many years, but you will look back and shudder to think how unengaged and uninterested in others you were. Those who have been on this journey for a while would give a hearty "Amen" to what I just shared.

In the next excerpt, the Lord gave me insights into how handling grief is a skill and not a problem to avoid or fight.

Dear Jesus,

I must confess, I've read that list of Paul's experiences before, but only for information. This time, I imagined how it must have felt to be whipped thirty-nine times. I thought about treading water in the ocean for twenty-four hours, desperately trying not to drown. I tried to picture how I would have felt when the stones pounded my body and I fell to the ground unconscious.

I've experienced suffering in my life but nothing like Paul. Thank You for giving me a larger view than my tiny world. It's so easy to focus only on my suffering when I'm grieving.

It would be an honor to learn the three goals that guided his life. If you are willing, I want to make them mine, too.

With my whole heart,

Your child

▼ ▼ ▼ ▼ ▼

Precious child,

I'm pleased to hear My word is becoming more than information. It is more living and active in your heart than you can imagine. Paul wrote his goals in a letter to the church at Philippi:

My goal is to know Him and the power of His resurrection and the fellowship of His sufferings, being conformed to His death ...

Philippians 3:10 (HCSB)

Before I share each goal, you need to understand what the English word "know" in Paul's letter means.

You can know rock climbing by reading about it in books and talking about it with rock climbers. You can also know rock climbing by fully experiencing it yourself—the sweat, muscle aches, rush of hanging from towering heights, and joy of reaching the summit. Paul doesn't seek to know about God, but to experience His presence, His power, and the fellowship of being with Him fully. Always remember ... knowing about Me merely informs you; experiencing My presence transforms you.

Goal #1: Know Me

Your first goal is to experience My presence. I have promised a special blessing to those like yourself who have never seen Me but still believe. Take heart! You are doing better at this than you think. The Holy Spirit is always working, even when you feel like you're coming up short.

It may surprise you to discover you have already been practicing this goal. The starting place for knowing Me is to take one day at a time. The righteous walk by faith and that means walking in the present. My presence transforms believers, enabling them to now wonder about their faith in the future or mull over unbelief in their past. They understand living in the past or the future are only tricks of Satan to distract them.

Think of a time when you ate lunch with someone who was distracted. You could tell he wasn't listening. His mind had drifted to a different time zone—the past or the future. Strengthening your connection with him was impossible because he wasn't in the present.

Walking with Me one day at a time helps you avoid making that mistake in our relationship. I am here for you now. Be here with Me now.

Everlasting life is an incredible dance of happiness and love you can enjoy only when you walk with Me in the present. Open your heart to Me and I will take away your sackcloth and clothe you with joy. You will find My joy to be your strength (Psalm 30:11).

Goal #2: Know the Power of My Resurrection

Your second goal is to experience the power of My resurrection. A good starting place is to ask the One who raised Me from the dead to help you pray. Prayer can be difficult when you are grieving. So, share your burdens with the Holy Spirit and ask the Comforter to help you.

Ask the Holy Spirit to restore the deep parts of your mind that have been wounded by death. Ask the Spirit to fill you with hope and power when you feel hopeless and powerless. Invite My Spirit into the deepest parts of your heart and rejoice when holy love, holy faith, and holy peace spring from your inner being.

At each stage of your life, My Spirit has taught you deeper truths about Me. The Comforter wants to teach you about heaven now. Study the Bible and read books about heaven by authors who follow Me. Heaven is the full expression of the power of My resurrection, so immerse your imagination in heaven and you will experience the Spirit's power over grief. You will discover never-ending hope as you learn the truth about where Holli lives now (Romans 15:13, Psalm 17:8).

Goal #3: Know the Fellowship of My Suffering

Your final goal is to embrace suffering with Me each day.

People wonder why there is suffering in the world. They question how good or powerful I am because of suffering. The answer isn't complicated ... the first man and woman disobeyed the Father, and all creation groans under the curse of sin as a result. Suffering is as common in a fallen world as the air we breathe.

No one likes to suffer. In fact, human nature avoids suffering at all costs. Fully human and divine, even I asked the Father the night before the Romans crucified Me if He could redeem the world without Me suffering. But there was not another way. So, I offered My life on the cross as a sacrifice for humanity's sins. Now everyone who believes in Me can experience everlasting love.

The chief question about suffering isn't "Why?" It is "What?" What are you going to do with the suffering in your life? Satan uses suffering to tempt people to rationalize their right to sin. He uses it to criticize My character. But I am working every circumstance in your life for good—even suffering. You choose if your suffering will honor Satan as a trophy for the kingdom of darkness or be a stepping-stone into My marvelous light.

Two types of people travel through life—people who have lost a loved one and people who have not. You instantly connect with people who are grieving because suffering draws people to one another. Likewise, you feel a deep love for those who understand you.

On the other hand, those who have never lost a close loved one can never understand what you are experiencing. In the same way, suffering helps you love Me well because you understand the depths of My love and sacrifice.

After you lose someone dear, you never look at My suffering on the cross the same again. I learned to love the Father with all My human heart, mind, soul, and strength through the suffering I experienced. The same is true for you. The purest water breaks through the hardest rock. The finest diamond forms by the greatest pressure underneath the earth. And the most precious heart to Me perseveres with love through suffering. That's what I did. With my help, you can do it too.

Follow these goals and you will do well,

Jesus

Friend, you have probably wondered many times since your loved one died what your next steps should be.

Early in your grief journey, God will give you small, simple goals because that is all you can manage. You will hear Him say goals like "get out of bed today," or "talk to a friend about your sorrow," or "don't try to hide your sorrow but ask for the help you need." You will notice He gives you the same goals repeatedly until they are easy for you to do and have become a part of your new normal. Just like repetition helps in physical therapy, God knows repetition is the key to grief therapy.

As time goes on, though, God will start to give you bigger goals. He will ask you to make bigger faith statements about what you can do in your life with Him. The smaller goals He gave at first will build a strong foundation of faith upon which these bigger goals can rest. This takes time, though.

We want to rush past our grief and get to the other side. But one key to the skill of grieving is being patient and letting the Holy Spirit bring about the healing in your life. I can't tell you how many people I've known who have tried to rush the journey and act like they were over their grief and ready to move on (I am one of them). After several months, however, they would be back at the support group having realized their foundation was still wobbly and they needed to take more time in their grief work.

Please remember that this whole practice of hearing from God and making faith statements has a purpose. Jesus wants the best for you and that is a life based on everlasting goals. That's how He lived His life and changed the world. That's how He wants us to live our lives as well. What I - and many before me - have found is that when you focus on these three everlasting goals, all the rest of your goals take care of themselves.

Live It Out: As you begin to make bigger lifetime goals, keep your focus on God's three everlasting goals.

▼ ▼ ▼ ▼ ▼

How do we make goals that are faith statements? We ask God a simple question each morning when we awake:

Lord, what are the three things you want me to do today?

When God shares His goals for us that day, we record them and commit to doing them as quickly as possible. Once we complete His goals, we are free to rest or ask for an extra goal. In the evening, we look at our list and talk to God about how our day went. He gives us wisdom when we fail and says "well done" when we have carried out what He gave us to do.

I know this skill will help you in your journey because it has helped me many times. Asking God for three faith statements each day for over 20 years guided me through the pain and fatigue of ankylosing spondylitis (AS). AS is a type of rheumatoid arthritis that affects the spine, rib cage, and hip joints. Most days I experienced pain levels or fatigue of seven or eight on a scale of ten. Struggling with pain while living overseas and surrounded by people who didn't know Jesus sometimes made life seem impossible. But asking God for three goals each day kept me close to Him and on the path of blessing.

I am thankful for how God has blessed my ministry in ways I could have never imagined, all because of asking God one simple question. And once again I found this question so important as I wept and trembled when I lost Holli.

Goals are the first part of the GROW plan because they start our journey through the valley of grief and keep us going. But these goals are not like the goals we have been taught to make all our lives. Creating goals that are faith statements after losing a loved one honors their memory and pleases God. And thankfully, it is not the size of our faith, but the size of God's love that brings healing and hope on our grief journey.

6

ROADBLOCKS ON THE JOURNEY

Jesus, I feel such absence, please be present.
I feel such loss, please be here.
I feel such sadness, please be my sanctuary.
I feel such pain, please be with me.
I feel such confusion, please be truth.
I feel such anger, please be peace.
I feel such hopelessness, please be promise.
I feel such emptiness, please be near.
Jesus, I feel such loneliness, please be beside me.
I feel such heartache, please be close.
I feel such doubt, please be faithfulness.
I feel such guilt, please lead me home.
The loss has consumed me. I come as I am.
Please be my everything. I just take your hand.
Amen.

- UNKNOWN

Walking beside Jesus through the valley of grief takes a long time, longer than any of us want. We move three steps forward and two back with no end in sight. The path is not straight but instead it is winding with many twists and turns. Just when we feel like we are doing well, a song plays on the radio or a memory of a special moment with our loved one washes over us. Just when we feel stronger, another holiday rolls around and we long for the way our life used to be.

Remember, the evil one doesn't play fair and will do anything to discourage you. One of the chief ways he does this is by putting obstacles on our path through the valley of grief that seem insurmountable. The good news is that Jesus has already defeated every obstacle we will ever face. We overcome our roadblocks not in our own power, but by the power of Jesus' blood on the cross. No roadblock can stand against His resurrection power.

We experience much distress when we lose a loved one and testimonies of God's faithfulness give us courage when we feel powerless and stuck. Thankfully, God's Word is full of the testimonies of people who have found Him trustworthy. God renews our confidence when we see how He has worked in the lives of others before us.

I was having coffee with a fellow grief traveler one day, and this friend recommended an approach to connecting with God that heals grief called *Immanuel Journaling*.[1] This style of journaling is based on Moses' and God's conversation at the burning bush:

> *Then the Lord said, "I have surely seen the affliction of my people who are in Egypt and have heard their cry because of their taskmasters. I know their sufferings, and I have come down to deliver them out of the hand of the Egyptians and to bring them up out of that land to a good and broad land, a land flowing with milk and honey..."*
>
> *Exodus 3:7-8 (ESV)*

God tells Moses that He has seen the Egyptians afflicting His people, He has heard their cries; He knows their sufferings, and He has come to deliver them.

Just as God saw His people suffering under the Egyptians, He sees your suffering under the weight of grief. He will hear your cries of loneliness. He will show you His plan to help you past your roadblocks.

While many obstacles can stand in our way through the valley of grief, the four most common are navigating holidays, memories of our loved one, feelings of loneliness, and depression. As you read the following letters between Jesus and me, you will notice the same pattern in His replies: seeing, hearing, knowing, and delivering. Let them be a guide to help you whenever you encounter a roadblock.

Holidays

I thought I was making great progress in my grief journey until the holidays arrived. Everything reversed and I returned to some of my deepest feelings of grief during Thanksgiving and Christmas that first year. Dread filled my heart thinking about how painful our traditions would be at every holiday forward. In some ways, the holidays felt like another funeral—the family gathered around the table, but Holli wasn't there because she had died. How many more funerals must we endure?

Grief work is emotionally draining and few of us have enough emotional energy to navigate the holidays alone. I found myself shuffling along, taking one difficult step after another, and trying to ignore all the joyful music. Christmas wasn't the greatest time of the year for me: Christmas was the most agonizing.

The holidays are such a grim time for those who grieve that GriefShare® has produced a special program to help members overcome this roadblock. I heartily recommend it as another resource for support.

Whether it's Thanksgiving and Christmas or Easter or the Fourth of July for you, the roadblock of the holidays hits hard again and again. I journaled a great deal as I grieved through the holidays, but the entry below has helped me the most. I pray it does the same for you.

Jesus,

How do people make it through their grief without You, Lord? I can't begin to imagine. What am I going to do about the holidays this year? I dread them more than anything I can remember in my life. How can I be happy when I'm so sad?

All the Joy is Gone,

Your Child

▼ ▼ ▼ ▼ ▼

Dear Child of God,

I see feelings of dread about the holidays smothering your heart. Your world is so different since Holli died and it's not easy to know the next step. I see you clench your teeth as you wrestle with an empty chair at the table. The holidays feel like a giant mountain you can't ignore and must climb. You are sure it is only a matter of time until you plummet off the highest cliff and fall to your death.

You fear the holidays will feel like her funeral all over again. I hear you telling yourself you don't have the emotional strength and it will hurt too much. I hear you saying you don't know how you will shop for presents without Holli. Your emotional tank is running close to empty, and it seems impossible to wait in shopping lines. And you dread answering questions about how you are doing.

I feel how much your heart aches right now and know this is hard. You wish your life could return to how it used to be. You worry about how the family will react to the holidays. You feel inadequate to face this challenge. The roadblock of the holidays is one of the biggest ones you will face, but know I am going to help you overcome it.

The holidays are important to you because you came from a broken family. You and Holli promised each other your family would reverse the curse. You dreaded the holidays after your parent's divorce, but by My grace, you and Holli changed the holidays into times of joy in your family. Because of Holli's death, you fear your family will slip back into the unsafe places you experienced when you were young—places that left you feeling anxious, empty, and unloved.

You should know that I have always enjoyed the holidays with you, Holli, and the children. I loved the candles, the worship, telling what you loved about one another, and remembering each year with an ornament. You always made it delightful to celebrate with you. Your love for one another and the way you welcomed My presence made it effortless to lavish My love on your whole household.

I'm proud of you for admitting how emotionally exhausted you are instead of just "pushing through." Even though you are struggling with your loss, you care more about the holidays not wounding your family. Confessing your weakness and My strength is a giant step toward healing. Admitting your need for Me opens your heart and your children's hearts to My conquering love.

Take heart, dear child. These first few holidays will be hard, but you will find a way to make them special again. You won't always be in deep sorrow at the foot of a hill called Golgotha. Holidays are coming when you will kneel beside a manger with kings and shepherds, listening to angels singing songs of praise.

You have already been practicing the skills needed to make it through the holidays. Create a checklist of what you can do realistically during this holiday. Take one day at a time. Don't be afraid to say you can't manage something if you feel overwhelmed. When you must pull away to regroup, let My grace and not your guilt rule the day.

Talk about the dreams you and Holli shared about the holidays with your children and ask everyone to help them come true. Ask your family to come together and help you make new traditions. Finally, let My light shine through your family like it always has. Even on the darkest night, you shine like stars in the sky.

I am with you,

Immanuel

Jesus said the truth sets us free. The truth is the holidays are going to be a roadblock you face regularly—not just the big ones, but the small ones too. You may never have had traditions for Memorial or Veteran's Day before, but the fact your loved one is not here to celebrate with you can send you in a tailspin. It's hard when friends invite you over for their barbeque and you feel like a fifth wheel.

Make a point to be honest about your struggle with the holidays. Set healthy boundaries with others and keep them. Share truthfully where you are in your grief journey. Be honest with yourself when you need to leave the present company, go to another room, and work through your sorrow. Honesty is the best policy as you deal with the roadblock of the holidays.

While it is true that you and the family will need to make new traditions, don't throw the old ones out too quickly. Find ways to alter important traditions without draining the meaning out of them. You are already grieving losing your loved one and don't need the added grief of surrendering traditions that mean a lot to you.

I found following the Lord's instructions to take one day at a time and create a checklist to be helpful. The roadblock of the holidays is huge, but you will make it through them. You will find new traditions and the day will come when your family talks about your loved one as if they were in the room instead of missing. Those will be precious moments because you will know God has delivered you from the hand of your oppressor.

Live It Out: Practice sharing honestly with yourself and others during holiday seasons. Sharing honestly is a sign of strength and not weakness. Let friends and family know you are still healing from your grief and cannot take part in the festivities as you did before. You need more rest and time alone. Maybe next year ...

Memories

We face the holidays a couple of times a year, but memories can overwhelm us on any given day. A song comes on the radio while you're driving to the store and all you can think of is dancing with her on your wedding day. The scent of fresh-cut grass fills the air on a Saturday afternoon; he always came in smelling like the lawn he kept so tidy. A friend from church delivers a meal and there are oatmeal raisin cookies for dessert—his favorite. And suddenly your heart rips open again.

The human mind doesn't simply stamp memories into its consciousness like typing letters on a keyboard records data in a computer. No, the human mind is more like making a home video. It records all the experiences and can play it back in theater surround sound again and again. This includes the good memories from that past that may now trigger sadness and sorrow as our loved one is missing. But this can also include vivid memories from the season of loss.

I can't tell you how many times I pled with Jesus to "turn off my mind." It seemed when one grief video stopped playing another instantly took its place. Sometimes I jumped in horror, other times my heart pounded from the drama, and the projector of my mind seemed stuck on the scene where Holli died. My mind played that scene in slow motion more times than I could count.

When the memories appeared unstoppable, God intervened. These letters from my journal are a testimony to how He sees us, hears us, and will work to deliver us.

Dear Jesus,

Please turn the memories off. Terrible images of Holli's illness play across the screen of my mind endlessly. This roadblock is way too big for me. What I would give to have just thirty minutes of peace in my troubled soul.

Hear my cry, Lord

Your Child

▼ ▼ ▼ ▼ ▼

Child of God,

My eyes are always on you. I see when torment engulfs your heart as memories flood your mind. I notice when tears fill your eyes or when you barely hold them back. I see the lump in your throat, and how hard it is to swallow.

I was listening when you told a friend you wished all your memories would stop so you could breathe again. Your cries for peace have reached My ears. You are always on My mind.

I understand your concerns about losing even more of Holli. You are afraid of forgetting who she was and don't want her love to become a distant memory. You want people to remember her and not go on as if she had never been alive. It scares you when you can't remember what she looked like, or what her voice sounded like.

You have endured significant suffering in your life, so remembering the good times with Holli is especially important to you. But you feel like Satan is using the bad memories to steal the good ones. You are afraid he is using the sad memories to plant lies in your heart. You hate his kingdom and feel the bad memories are slowly sucking you into darkness.

I want you to know I am the Light of the world, and I am still with you. One reason I enjoy our time together is because of how vulnerable you are with Me—a little sincerity goes a long way. It's refreshing to talk to one of My children who is honest about how they feel. I look forward to our talks every time.

I'm proud of you for sharing your doubts. My Word says to show mercy on those who doubt (Jude 22). Doubts destroy the fabric of your life one strand at a time and are terrifying. But I care deeply for you and am using everything in your life to make you a whole person—even your doubts. Your doubts scare you, but they don't scare Me.

Take heart, dear child. I'm not going to let you forget Holli—she means too much to both of us. I promise memories of the good times you shared will return. Remembering Holli won't always cripple you emotionally. You are under major spiritual reconstruction right now and few parts of your life look the same. One day, however, you will be healed, have hope, and see everything more clearly.

When you enter heaven, you will hear Holli's voice calling you, more beautiful than you remember. Now she speaks from a heart of abundance. You will dance a jig when you hear her pure, sweet voice and know all the prayers you prayed together for her deliverance have been answered forever.

My love conquers all,

Jesus

After a while, all the memories of your loved one will not be painful but precious to you. I remember an older man telling me those words early in my grief journey and I didn't believe him. But it is true. Several years into the journey, the grieving videos have slowly been replaced with grateful videos. I'm grateful for the memories we made together. I'm thankful for the different memories that family members share giving us all a fuller picture of who Holli was and is.

Jesus is not only the memory-maker, but He is also the memory-taker. As you come before His throne, share the memories that are terrorizing you and imagine Him taking them and throwing them as far as the east is from the west. In the fog of grief, we struggle to believe our painful memories will ever stop. But they are not as strong as our Savior. He is renewing our minds and the more memories we have stored, the more time it takes.

One day, friend, you will use your memories as weapons against the evil one. He seems to be winning now, but what Satan has meant for evil, God is turning to good.

Live It Out: Video stores used to put a sticker on videos that said, "Be Kind. Rewind." Make a point today of being kind to yourself as you rewind and view old memories. You are not your memories, but a child of the living King. Let His life within you—not your past—define you.

Loneliness

Memories are fleeting and the holidays come once a year, but loneliness feels like it will last a lifetime. Loneliness causes widows and widowers to make poor decisions, settle for second best, and doubt God's loving care. Been there, done that.

We punish our most hardened criminals with solitary confinement. Too often, the loneliness we feel after our loved one has died seems like God is punishing us. Grief can make the most popular person at a party feel like they are alone in a dungeon.

Answers to loneliness abound. Some people say, "You need to get a dog." Others say, "Pour yourself into your work so you won't feel the loneliness." Still others say, "You need a new hobby or sport. Why don't you start a basket-weaving class down at the local college." If well-meaning people have given you this advice, you know how it only makes you feel lonelier and more misunderstood.

So, what should we do when loneliness overwhelms us? This is a roadblock I continue to work on with Jesus' help, but here are some insights He gave me early in my grief journey that I pray will help you defeat this formidable foe.

Dear Jesus,

I'm so lonely and I don't know what to do. Can you help?

Sincerely,

Your Child

▼ ▼ ▼ ▼ ▼

Child of Mine,

I see you struggling with being single. Holli's death has changed all your friendships and you aren't sure where you stand with most people. It's not easy to become a single person after thirty years of marriage. I see your shoulders slump when you think about walking through the rest of life alone.

I hear you saying your loneliness is not fair. You and Holli had something special that others cannot understand. You mutter under your breath when you see couples arguing in public. I've heard you ask Me to end your singleness because it is not good for man to be alone. Loneliness is not a big boulder blocking the road, but more like a giant rock that has tumbled off a cliff and flattened you.

Fallen people have found it impossible to experience healthy relationships since Adam and Eve sinned in the garden. I understand how you feel because I experienced loneliness when I walked in this broken world. I know your agony because My heart ached the same way on the cross. I sacrificed myself in place of your everlasting loneliness so you could have My everlasting happiness.

You are fervent about ending your loneliness because of how relational I made you. You love to be with people and feeling disconnected from others makes you wither. Hanging out with believers is like living water to you. You are sad because Holli's death has meant the end of important friendships and it feels like your well is drying up.

Loneliness has a way of eating away at your self-confidence too. So, I want you to know I enjoy being with you. You are not struggling with loneliness because something is wrong with you. A pandemic of lonely people covers the earth today. Sadly, countless people are living their entire lives like they are in quarantine.

You haven't noticed all the lonely, isolated people before. You never considered the multitudes who live by themselves because of death, divorce, or other difficulties. Now you find yourself asking Me to give the gift of life-giving friendships. I'm proud of how you are trans-forming your loneliness into a passion to help others.

Let loneliness motivate you to develop deeper friend-ships. Talk with your friends about the ingredients of healthy relationships. Invite Me to share in every conversation. Use this time to work on the unhealthy places in your own life.

You believe loneliness will follow you all the days of your life, but that simply is not true. A drought causes trees to sink their roots deeper into the soil and become stronger. In the same way, I am using loneliness to strengthen your commitment to love others and Me well. I am not punishing you but preparing you for a plentiful harvest.

My Love Conquers All,

Jesus

Just like wolves single out the weakest animal in the herd, the evil one wants to put us in a constant state of loneliness so he can devour us whenever he wants. He whispers in your ear when you are out in public that you are "different" and that adds to your loneliness. But God has put many people in your life who love you and are concerned about what you are going through. There are people who care. They can be busy with their own lives, but they do care.

Try to reframe your feelings of loneliness as time alone. Women and men have crafted the greatest music, art, and writing when they were alone. Some of the greatest prayers and spiritual thoughts have come when people were alone. Many of the discoveries that have helped people the most occurred when people separated themselves for a time so their creativity would not be distracted.

Most of us are not great musicians, artists, authors, researchers, or discoverers. But you are a genius when it comes to you. You know the places in your life that are strong and the ones that need work. You are on a grief journey because your whole world has changed. Leverage this journey to make the changes within yourself that will make you a healthier person. Then, whether you marry again or not, you will have found contentment; and contentment with godliness is a true treasure.

Live It Out: Although we miss our loved ones, they want us to use the change in our life to become healthier, stronger people. They have an everlasting view now and see their death as a stepping-stone for us, not a tombstone. What little step can you take today toward becoming a stronger person?

Depression

As the fog settled in my mind after the first few months, the sky was always full of the dark clouds of depression. I could not find any color in the world—everything was black, white, and a thousand shades of gray.

Almost ten percent of the population has a major depressive episode each year according to Johns Hopkins Medicine.[2] Eighteen percent of adults suffer from panic disorders. Life is tough and many people are barely making it through. Add losing a loved one to the mix and you have a recipe even double chocolate brownies can't fix.

Grief amplifies everything in our life, including depression. Though we may look like we are doing fine, many of us are carrying a heavy load because of the trauma we have experienced in this broken world. Depression is a silent pandemic that our culture has only recently begun to recognize. In my experience, and that of many people I know who have lost a loved one, the roadblock of depression comes often and only grows stronger if we don't address it in our lives.

I wrote this journal entry at a deep time of depression and pray God uses it to pull you out of a dark place of discouragement when you need it.

Dear Jesus,

I'm stuck and I don't know which way to turn. The smallest event can set me on a downward spiral of sorrow. When will this emotional pain end? If I could give up and admit defeat, I think I would.

Beaten and bruised,

Your Child

▼ ▼ ▼ ▼ ▼

Child of God,

I see the battle you are fighting every day. You wake up in the morning with your fists clenched, ready to fight your grief for the millionth time. Fear makes your chest feel heavier and heavier. You try to steady yourself and brace against more setbacks. I see you sit motionless in your favorite chair hoping the poisonous snake of depression will slither by without seeing you.

I hear you questioning your thinking often. You thought I would heal Holli on earth, but I didn't. You thought you and Holli would retire together, but you won't. You thought she would be the greatest grand-mother ever, but she isn't here for your grandson. So many disappointments have made your voice uncertain when you talk to others and to Me.

I understand how you could feel trapped by a grief journey that seems like it will never end. Death has beaten you down like the cruel people who abuse animals. Death has thrown you into a cage of helplessness and convinced you escaping is impossible. You feel stuck and like giving up.

Breaking free from grief is impossible on your own— but you are not alone. I came to set the captives free. We are friends and I'm not going anywhere. I am the conquering King of Kings and Lord of Lords. I live in you, and everything bows in reverence to My authority. Because I am with you, no cage in the world can hold you.

I am proud of you for enduring hardship as My soldier. Even though you are hurting more than any other time in your life, you are still fighting the good fight. You put on the armor I have given you and seek My marching orders every day. You continue to stand against Satan when he tries to discourage you by reminding you of mistakes in your past.

Take heart, precious child. I know I made you from dust. Don't look at the minuscule number of mistakes in your life and paint your future with that dark color. Instead, rest in the multitude of good works you and I have done together—a masterpiece of mercy filled with gorgeous colors and textures.

Someday, Holli will show you the places where your colors and her colors connected and blended in harmony. She has hung both your paintings in the entryway of her mountain mansion. She enjoys having friends over and

*praising Me with the story of your lives together. That's
right, I'm not the only one proud of you in heaven!*

*Soldier of the Living God, you are never helpless
when I am on your side. Call on Me and I will show
you great and mighty wonders you cannot begin to
imagine. I parted the Red Sea when Moses prayed. I
stopped the sun when Joshua prayed. I sent rain when
Elijah prayed. I fed a widow and her son when Elija
prayed. And I brought My people out of captivity
when Daniel prayed. Nothing is too difficult for Me.*

My Love Conquers All,

Jesus

Depression is one of the favorite snares of the evil one.
First, he accuses you of not doing or being enough. Second,
he destroys your confidence and floods your heart with
discouragement. Third, he steals your self-image and
tells you someone who feels so discouraged must be a
bad person. Fourth, he tries to kill your connection with
God and make you feel worthless.

The fruit of this cycle is an inability to feel good about
life or desire to do anything. When you get to that place,
the evil one can start the vicious cycle again and take
you down even further. If you suffer from depression,
you should know that many of the people God has used
the most throughout history struggled with depression
like you do.

Because the evil one is the father of lies, the chief weapon
we wield against him is truth. I don't know anyone who
has overcome depressive episodes in their life without the
help of a friend or counselor. We need a brother or sister
in Christ who listens to us share our struggles vulnerably

and then shares the truth of God's grace, mercy, and forgiveness with us. Not someone who mindlessly shares memorized Bible verses, but a friend who speaks to us with the tenderness of our crucified Savior—the One who knows we are but dust.

Live It Out: Depression is like the warning light on your car—it is a sign that something needs to be changed or fixed. It is not a sign of weakness or that you are defective. Please talk to your pastor or a professional Christian counselor if you can't resolve the warning light yourself. You are a blessing to the family of God, friend, and we need you back.

▼▼▼▼▼

The four largest roadblocks we face on our journey of grief are the holidays, memories of our loved one, soul-crushing loneliness, and dark episodes of depression. They are not the only roadblocks we run up against, however. Each person has a unique journey of grief filled with roadblocks specific to their life experiences. The good news is the skills we learn to overcome the biggest roadblocks also work on all the others.

Don't be surprised if you meet the same roadblock again on a different part of your journey. The problem with roadblocks is you never see them coming. That's why one of the questions we can ask ourselves each day is:

Is there a roadblock in my way that I need to work on today?

When you face the same roadblock, thank God that you have already learned the skills to overcome it, and praise Him that you have another opportunity to strengthen your grief skills. Easier said than done sometimes, I know, but it is the best place to be with God's help.

In the "Goal" section of the GROW plan, I shared how asking God the simple question "What are the three things You want me to do today?" acted like a flashlight directing me through the darkness in my grief journey. At first, God in His wisdom shared very small action steps for me to take. The steps had to be small because I did not have the strength to overcome even the smallest roadblock early in my grief journey. Just getting out of bed or going to work took enormous effort.

Little by little, Jesus increased the scope of the goals He gave me. Now that I was faithfully following His goals for me each day, Jesus began to include tasks that taught me how to overcome the roadblocks in my grief journey.

Every day that I took a sledgehammer to the roadblock in front of me, I noticed Jesus was beside me pounding the roadblock with His sledgehammer too. And His swing was doing far more than mine could have ever done in a lifetime.

Even though I had doubted Him and questioned His character, God continued to put salve on my wounds and sing songs of deliverance over me. Even though the journey seemed impossible to me so many times, He could see the progress every day and knew I was much further along than I realized. I was looking at how far I had come, He pointed to how deep I had become.

Endnotes

1 Joyful Journey: Listening to Immanuel. E James Wilder III, Anna Kang, John Loppnow, and Sungshim Loppnow. Presence and Practice, 2020.

2 https://www.hopkinsmedicine.org/health/wellness-and-prevention/mental-health-disorder-statistics

7

OWNING MY GRIEF

*Father, you tell us all things work for good. I
don't see it right now. I don't know how sickness
and death can work for my good. I don't have
your eyes in this situation. But I do trust you.
I've seen you take the most difficult, painful
circumstances and use them for good. I want to
believe you will take this year and do the same.
Help my unbelief. In Jesus' name,*

- DENA MARTIN

Masons build the largest cathedrals one brick at a time. Rebuilding your life after losing your soulmate is no different. When you ask Jesus, "What are your three goals for me today?" He hands you three bricks. Completing the goals puts the bricks in place.

Day by day you will start to notice that Jesus is your cornerstone, and He is helping you build a new normal—a new life—a new temple to His glory. Slowly mosaics of faith, hope, and love begin to form in the walls. Then you see arches that display the glory of knowing Him, the power of His resurrection, and the fellowship of His suffering.

Each of us will walk our own unique journey through the valley of grief. But as I've said before, that does not mean we walk alone. It's not simply nice to have a friend to talk with or encourage you. Connecting to others is a necessary skill to master when we are hurting and want to hide in our grief. God sends these connections in different ways, at different times in the journey. Some, like a GriefShare® group, may be with us for a longer part of the walk. Others we will meet along the way. And some may be in the testimonies of those who have shaped and inspired us from seasons past.

God especially blessed my grief journey by giving me a new friendship with a pastor in New York. He had read about Holli passing away in my book *Fear is a Liar* and reached out to me by email. Though I was still in "the dark night of my soul" and didn't always return emails, the Spirit granted me the grace to respond. My friend wrote that he had lost his wife of thirty years to COVID-19 the previous week, so we set up a FaceTime meeting for the next Tuesday.

Over the next year, we shared our struggles and comforted each other every Tuesday afternoon—two devastated brothers drowning in sorrow. God had thrown each of us a life preserver and pulled us closer and closer to shore every time we talked. We both helped each other work through the "Own It" stage of the GROW plan.

In the same way Jesus sent me a friend on my journey, you are not alone on this journey. There are those around you who love you and want to see you grow and thrive. We have a God who understands our sorrow, who promises to comfort the brokenhearted, and who sends others to be with us on this path. He is also a God who shows us the way forward. He has connected you and me, two weary travelers in the valley of grief, through this book.

As our skills in setting goals and overcoming roadblocks begin to become familiar, Jesus will lead us to the next skill—Owning It. God loves us too much to leave us in our brokenness, but for us to move forward, we must surrender our own attempts to manage our lives. We must own the fact that the coping strategies we are using just don't work. We "own" our mistakes and humbly ask God to forgive and restore us.

"Owning it" is not a skill you have to master all at once. Rather, this is a posture of openness to let God open our eyes to our own failures and teach us His way. As God shows you it's time to go deeper, you may begin to add a daily question:

God, what do I need to own today?

This humble approach to life is a skill we can build. But as we are on the grief journey, some of the most common places we need to own are doubt, loneliness, repentance, and hope. Take each area as God shows you it is time. For me, the "O" part of the GROW plan was the hardest yet most rewarding step in my journey through the valley of grief.

Owning Doubt

It's not difficult to understand why we struggle with doubt after our soulmate passes away. Processing the death of a loved one makes us question what we believe about God. Our loved one suffered, so we wonder why God allows people to suffer. Our loved one died of the malpractice of a doctor, so we wonder why God doesn't bring justice. The more our questions go unanswered, the more our doubts grow.

We also struggle with doubt because our culture believes Jesus isn't the only way to heaven. Many people today believe all religions will reach the top of a mountain someday and discover they are the same. As a result, our culture says people who believe *only* in Jesus are narrow-minded, dogmatic, and self-righteous—bad people. No one wants to be a bad person, so we swim against a strong current of doubt every day.

We would stay lost in doubt if God had not given us the Holy Spirit to reveal truth. The Holy Spirit says Jesus is the door, so any spiritual truths in other religions are merely signs pointing to the door of the true God. The Spirit says Jesus is the light of the world. Other religions are like a candle: at best, help for peering through a dark night, but certainly not the sun that rises every day.

The Holy Spirit also declares that God is the most trustworthy person in the universe. Hundreds of prophecies in the Bible prove His faithfulness. Millions of believers from every nation testify to His goodness and mercy. Both of us have seen God work in our lives many times, too.

It's human nature to forget the good in our past when we suffer from the bad in the present. Please avoid that trap. Being grateful for the past is the key to overcoming doubt. God grants us peace today when we thank Him for what He did yesterday (Philippians 4:6-7).

I know how hard it is to be thankful when you are grieving. We have lost a precious gift God gave us. I've been walking through the valley a while now and some days still grumble instead of being grateful. Only God can give us the strength we need to give thanks when we don't feel like it.

How can we become grateful in our grief? Build your "be thankful" muscle by starting with the easy weights. For one minute, practice thanking God for small non-emotional items like a meal, your clothes, or a warm bed to sleep in at night. When you are ready, practice giving God thanks for bigger unemotional items in your life. Try giving thanks for five minutes. Thank Him for your house, your favorite park, or a beautiful sunrise in the morning.

As God leads, move forward by thanking Him for small emotional events in your life: coffee with a friend, a phone call with your children, or a day with your grandchild. Be patient with yourself. Developing a thankful heart while you are grieving takes time. But it's worth it. See if you can work toward ten minutes of being grateful for the small emotional events in your life.

Finally, ask the Holy Spirit to help you give thanks as you walk through the big emotional experiences of your life. Be grateful for your wedding, the birth of a child, or other precious memories with your loved one. I'm not suggesting you thank God for your partner's death, but all the times you had together. By this time, you will be an expert at the art of thanksgiving.

Live It Out: Spend the right amount of time for you to build your "thankful" muscle today. Thanksgiving helps us doubt our doubts. The more grateful we are, the more hope we feel. And the more hope we feel, the more our doubts disappear.

Owning Loneliness

Struggling with loneliness is normal in our grief journey. When we lose someone close, we also lose a companion, a confidant, and a friendship that had significant meaning in our lives. If the loved one you lost was your spouse, it can be an even bigger struggle because multiple friendships changed as soon as your spouse passed away. All our married friends and the couples we shared friendship with are still couples, yet we're suddenly single. You might feel like an awkward teenager when they strike up conversations about their spouses. What used to be dinner together as couples can now leave you feeling like the third wheel. In my experience, loneliness is the biggest challenge someone faces when they lose a loved one.

Before we talk about "owning" your loneliness, I want to make sure you don't think your struggle with being alone is because there is something wrong with you. People enjoy being with you and want to hear what you have to say. The issue is the playing field has changed for all your friends because of your loved one's death. Everyone is uncertain how to adjust to the new "rules" and we all feel awkward … not just you.

For several weeks after your loved one's died, you needed time alone to decompress and sort out what had happened. You were figuring out new routines and struggling with intense sorrow. You needed to visit with friends but were uncomfortable sharing too much because you might lose control of your emotions and start crying. People gave you the space you needed, but this also weakened your connection to them.

You discovered how needy you were as you walked through the first year of grief. It's hard to admit we are needy and realize no one can meet all the needs in our heart. If we talk about our grief too much with friends, we feel even more needy. But not sharing our needs weakens our social network even further. Our friends want to know practical ways they can help us. They want to fulfill Jesus' command to love others by loving us. Not sharing our needs only further worsens our loneliness.

When we grieve, it is easy to think "I'll reconnect with people after I get stronger." That approach doesn't work, though. The main way God strengthens and encourages us is through conversations with others. Focusing *solely* on our needs always ends in a lonely wilderness filled with howling coyotes and venomous snakes.

When I struggle with loneliness, I remember that Jesus understands how I feel. He knows the pain in my soul and the fear of being abandoned forever. I know He understands because Jesus cried out from the cross, "My God, My God, why have you abandoned me." Jesus is the Lord and the Lover of My Soul. He cares about the loneliness I feel and will help me when I ask for His aid.

The next time you are lonely, picture yourself meeting Jesus in a quiet place and sitting on a bench together. Lean over, whisper in His ear, and tell Him about the pain and fear that loneliness is causing in your life. Thank Him for understanding and for the promise He will never abandon you. Listen to the compassion in His voice as He responds.

Strengthening your connection to Jesus eases loneliness, but it's not the complete solution. God created us to be in community. It takes a village to help someone overcome their grief. Someone in the village needs to step forward and volunteer to jump-start friendships again. And the only person who can do that is you.

Thankfully, correcting the causes of loneliness only requires two skills: faith and initiative. Exercising faith means we stop focusing on what we don't have. Instead, we look forward to what we *will* have by God's grace. We celebrate the friends God will bring into our life instead of mulling over our loneliness.

Taking the initiative to make new friends can be scary, especially after a long interruption in relationships. But bravely taking that first step out the door pleases God, and He rewards our initiative. He knows how hard this is for us.

The good news? No one is better than the Holy Spirit at bringing friends together. The Spirit has already been working in your life and your future friends' lives too. In fact, some of the best friends you will have in this life are yet to come.

Live It Out: Healing in our grief journey comes when we own the fact that part of our loneliness is because we expect others to come to us. We are waiting for others to cure our feelings of isolation. Take the initiative today to call or visit someone you haven't seen in a while. Whether you meet them in person or online, ask the Holy Spirit to show you ways to love your friend well.

Owning Suffering

The other day, the Lord showed me that I was seeking happiness the same way the world does. I believed my grief would end when my life returned to being easy, more predictable, and less stressful. That's what our culture says happiness looks like but we both know counting on earth-based circumstances is a blind alley.

It's easy to slip into the same thinking in our walk with Jesus. I follow Him because He makes me more comfortable, blesses me with more money, and makes my life less stressful. If my circumstances are good, God loves me. If they are bad, God isn't very happy about something.

Even though I knew better, too much of my grief journey felt like I was in the second group—I had failed God somehow and He was angry. I was looking at my circumstances and not my Savior. What a difference it would have made if I had gazed at His dazzling radiance and opened my heart to His merciful love. Instead, I chose to look at the dreary storm clouds and wallow in self-pity.

I think you would agree that we talk about suffering for Jesus, but usually do all we can to avoid it. As a result, we are unprepared to face suffering when it comes—and trials always show up in a sinful world. We view pain as punishment from God, rather than an opportunity to experience more of His presence. We are uncomfortable with the thought that growing closer to Jesus sometimes means suffering with Him.

Talking about suffering, I must confess that crying doesn't come easy for me. I didn't cry when my parents divorced or when Holli's first pregnancy ended in a miscarriage. I wanted to ... I just couldn't. All the tears of all the years were bottled up inside me.

I knew my inability to cry was a problem after Holli died, so I decided to figure out a way to make myself cry. The best solution I found was watching "America's Got Talent" videos on YouTube, especially the golden buzzer episodes. Yeah, I know. It's cheesy, but it worked.

One singer who made me weep was a petite young woman who called herself Nightbirde. She had an angelic face that radiated sincerity and hope. Before she sang, the frail thirty-year-old talked about battling cancer for several years and said the doctors had given her a two-percent chance of living ... but that was better than zero percent. Her spunk amazed me and the judges.

Nightbirde then sang one of the most tender and honest songs I've ever heard. I cried and cried for the first time in many years. Through my tears I prayed:

Oh God, she is so much worse off than I am. I'm sorry for how privileged I have acted—like you owe me anything. I've complained about how you have treated me. I've spoken to you like a spoiled child. I am your servant, not the other way around. Please forgive me. Lord Jesus, have mercy on me, a sinner.

After she finished, the judges asked Nightbirde how she could have such a good attitude in the face of her prognosis. She said, "You can't wait until life isn't hard anymore before you decide to be happy."

May we embrace our suffering and let God have His perfect work in us. May we see suffering with Jesus as a gift and not a curse. May God's love flow out of our suffering hearts to those who feel pain, even as love flowed from Jesus' heart to the entire world. May we always be wounded healers like our Master.

Live It Out: We don't get a "get out of jail free" card just because we have lost someone we love. Think of situations during your grief journey when you have hurt others.

Ask the Lord to give you tears of remorse and a heart to own your sins and make things right. Grief work is hard enough without carrying tons of guilt too.

Owning Hope

Have you ever driven a car and suddenly realized you couldn't remember the previous five minutes of your trip? That's what it's like to be conscious and unconscious at the same time. I must admit I've been spiritually unconscious too often in my grief journey. It's easy when we are spiritually unconscious to put our spiritual life on autopilot. It's hard to admit we have traveled another day unconscious—not giving God a second thought.

I'm spiritually unconscious when I believe working hard or pleasing people will give me what I want in life. I'm unconscious when I try to be perfect so God will love me or when I overthink the future to control others. I may look like I'm awake, but I am not. Somewhere deep inside, I have placed my hope in idols that can not hear or speak. They have put me to sleep, and I am living in a dream world.

Unconscious people dream of a life with no family problems. A home where peace always reigns, and children never misbehave. They dream of a life with no problems with their friends—a wonderful place where everyone is close and never gossips or criticizes one another. They dream of no financial problems–a life where they win the lottery and go on endless shopping sprees. All these dreams are not reality, though. They are just pipe dreams.

Spiritually unconscious people try to solve their problems by dreaming about the outward aspects of their lives. They focus on external elements like power, reputation, money, and possessions. Spiritually conscious people, on the other hand, are not tempted by pipe dreams. Conscious people know the answer is within them—only the Holy Spirit is wise and strong enough to solve the problems of a world bursting with broken people.

Jesus promised rivers of living water would flow from everyone who believes in Him. The Bible explains these rivers are the Holy Spirit whom Jesus has given to live within us. You and I need to make the journey to the wellspring of the Spirit's presence every day and it starts with prayer.

As I come before God in prayer, He is my hiding place and deliverer. Life stands still as I bask in the Spirit's love and find the healing and hope I have yearned for.

I begin my journey of prayer marching past the taunts of the evil one and his minions. Then I start the descent to the center of my soul, leaving insecurities behind as I go even deeper, past shame and the people I have wounded—people who deserved better from me. God has forgiven me, but too often I struggle to walk in that forgiveness.

Halfway through the journey, I walk tearfully past thirty hospitalizations as a sickly child. Deeper still, I wince as I move past struggles with chronic pain and stiffness the past two decades. I weep softly as I move deeper still—slowly passing memories of Holli suffering and taking her final breath.

Deeper and deeper I travel until I am close to my inner-most being. Then, I hear a small quiet voice calling. A voice so beautiful it gives the weakest parts of me hope. A voice so strong I know nothing could ever separate me from God's love.

Finally, I walk up to a small wellspring of living water and the Spirit gently whispers:

Welcome home, child. I have been waiting for you. Lay your burdens down and find rest for your soul. We can talk or sit here quietly together. Whatever you need. I want to be with you. Forever. I am never going to let you go.

I am not sharing the pipe dreams of a spiritually unconscious person, friend. I am sharing the real hopes of someone who is spiritually conscious because I believe in Jesus; the hopes of someone who can face the future because Jesus lives in my heart. His living water is waiting for you, too.

Live It Out: Picture your own journey to the center of your soul as you pray today. What good events in your life do you see? What difficult parts of your life do you ponder? When you finally arrive at the center of your being, spend time with Jesus there. Only Jesus can give us a hope that endures, but we must take responsibility for receiving hope from Him and carrying it back into our daily lives.

▼▼▼▼▼

"Owning It" is the most difficult but most rewarding step in our grief journey because it is human nature for us to blame someone else when we are struggling with problems. God is to blame when I doubt because He didn't do what I thought He should do. Others are to blame when I'm lonely because they aren't reaching out to me as they should. I acted rudely because I'm having a hard time grieving, and you should overlook my offense.

And I don't have hope because of the culture I live in or because of toxic events in my past.

Blame is always a shell game to cover sin, though. The "Own It" step reminds us that we are fallen people who need God's help. But it also reminds us that He is rich in mercy and forgiveness. God constantly seeks an emotionally healthy relationship with us. And He loves us too much to allow us to try to cover our own sin.

Losing someone can take us to a deeper level spiritually when we face the truth we have not been as honest with ourselves, others, or God as we have pretended to be. Grief can be a gift to a deeper and more satisfying life if we let it. But only if we "own" our doubts, our loneliness, our sins, and our lack of hope. For it is only the humble and broken person that God raises up to new life.

8

WALKING WITH JESUS

Father, grant me gospel joy; help me to rejoice in Christ even as I grieve. Envelope me with the peace and comfort only you can provide.

As the days move into months, may this burden lessen. As the months move to years, use me to encourage and bless someone else who must walk a similar path.

Help me to point them to you as the God of all comfort. I know that you are always with me and that your love never ceases. Help me to find refuge in you and nowhere else.

- CHRISTINA FOX

Jesus gave us glimpses of what heaven is like during His earthly ministry. He cast out demons because heaven is a place where people have been delivered from evil. He healed the sick because there is no sickness in heaven. He showed the most offensive sinner God's grace and forgiveness because heaven overflows with God's love and mercy.

In his books *The Great Divorce* and *The Last Battle*, C.S. Lewis described our existence here on earth as "living in the shadowlands." When Holli passed away, I finally understood what Lewis meant. Losing a loved one forced me to recognize I had been walking in the shadowlands all my life. This world is merely a shadow of heaven—a place more stunning than we can imagine.

Life on earth is tough. It is full of pain, and sickness, and brokenness, and Satan is happy to remind us of this all the time. Do you remember how Satan tried to fill me with doubt and despair? How he whispered lies that I was doomed to this pain forever, that I was too weak to weather this storm, and that heaven wasn't real? The enemy takes advantage of the brokenness in this world to keep us confused and separated from God's love.

But even this doesn't surprise the Father. It saddens Him. But it does not surprise Him. It is precisely why He planned to send Jesus to earth to walk with us, speak with us, and finally die for us. One day God will renew and restore everything because of the power of the cross.

Until then, how do we live in the shadowlands? Thankfully, Jesus has shown us. The book of Matthew tells us how just before the start of Jesus' ministry, God sent Him out into the desert to fast for 40 days. Satan followed him, tempting Jesus with twisted doubts and lies. At every attempt to bring Him down, Jesus fought back with truth—God's truth. And then Satan left Him.

We are in a battle here, my friend, and grief is the fiercest battlefield. We must fight back when Satan tries to hit us with his blows. There are five key truths from God we can hold onto. They are our weapons. They are our promises that Jesus is with us here in the shadowlands. They are our guideposts on how to navigate life well on this side of heaven.

My True Identity

The self-help section in bookstores has always attracted me. I enjoy reading books that give advice on how to be a healthier, more authentic person. Judging from the number of self-help books published each year, I'm not alone. All of us seek healing from the emotional wounds in our lives. Deep in our hearts, we know our lives could be so much richer than the ones we are living.

When Holli died, I lost my sense of identity. I was no longer married but had become a single parent. Previously, I did everything with a partner but now I did everything alone. Most of the dreams I had for later in my life included Holli and no longer could happen. Losing a loved one after thirty years of marriage makes you ask, "Who am I?"

Maybe you lost a child and your identity as a parent has been severed. Maybe you spent years giving your time as a caregiver for a parent or sibling. Now that they're gone, who are you? When we lose someone close, the way we fit into the world around us changes and that rocks our identity.

On top of that, the emotions of grief make us feel like a different person. Sadness, fear, and anger act like playground bullies, taunting and kicking us when we are feeling down. When we start doing better, they question why we are letting ourselves feel good. The emotional roller coaster ride leaves us exhausted and wondering who we are.

In contrast, Jesus knew who He was. He knew where He had come from, what His mission was, and where He was going.

DEATH IS A LIAR

Jesus wasn't controlled recklessly by His emotions but righteously by the Holy Spirit. He did not lean on His own understanding (limited by the Incarnation) but sought boundless wisdom from the Father of Lights.

The night before His crucifixion, Jesus asked the Father to give His glory to all who believed in Him. God answered Jesus' prayer and has placed His glory in us. His glory shines in these earthly pots, so the world knows it is His glory, and not ours.

> *But we all, with unveiled face, beholding as in a mirror the glory of the Lord, are being transformed into the same image from glory to glory, just as by the Spirit of the Lord.*
>
> *2 Corinthians 3:18 (NKJV)*

When you see the glory of a person, you see their essence. God's glory has changed us into new people. He has made us whole by His resurrection power deep within our souls. We have confidence because God has filled us with His glory.

We know we are His.

> *See how very much our Father loves us, for he calls us his children, and that is what we are!*
>
> *1 John 3:1 (NLT)*

We know where we have come from.

> *But God, being rich in mercy, because of the great love with which he loved us, even when we were dead in our trespasses, made us alive together with Christ—by grace you have been saved ....*

Ephesians 2:4-5 (ESV)

And we know where we are going.

> *God raised us from death to life with Christ Jesus, and he has given us a place beside Christ in heaven. God did this so that in the future world he could show how truly good and kind he is to us because of what Christ Jesus has done.*

Ephesians 2:6-7 (CEV)

No matter what happens along the way, your identity is secure in Him.

Live It Out: A great cloud of witnesses in heaven surround us and rejoices to see us move from glory to glory. They know our journey is hard—it was hard for them too. If we could hear them, I believe they would tell us:

• Keep believing and trust God
• Keep hoping and don't sweat the small stuff
• Keep loving and work on the things you can control
• Keep calm and carry on

Ask God to show you how following the four statements above would increase your confidence and self-esteem during your grief journey.

Right Relationships

Jesus and His disciples had come back to Jerusalem and were walking through the temple courts. Jesus often walked and talked, teaching as he went. On this day, many of the religious leaders came to listen and to question him. A lawyer heard the debates and then asked his own question, "Of all the commandments, which is the most important?" Jesus said:

The most important commandment is this:

"Listen, O Israel! The Lord our God is the one and only Lord. And you must love the Lord your God with all your heart, all your soul, all your mind, and all your strength. The second is equally important: Love your neighbor as yourself."

No other commandment is greater than these.

Mark 12:29-30 (NLT)

We walk best through the shadowlands when we put God first and treat others the same way we treat ourselves.

Most of the relationship issues we face occur because of one of three reasons: God is not first in our life, we love ourselves *more* than others, or we love ourselves *less* than others. Choosing any one of these scenarios is living out of balance and sets us up for relational and spiritual disaster.

Popular books in our culture encourage us to be self-sufficient and not depend on others for success. They tell us to analyze our abilities and choose careers that match our strengths. Gurus say to follow our dreams, no matter the cost, and make false promises that if you think the right way you will grow rich. The problem with this approach is we are loving *ourselves* more than others.

Losing a loved one cuts through these ideas like a buzz saw. We realize a life solely driven by our needs and wants is an empty life. We understand that we have said our connection to God and others is important but too often allowed our ambitions and passions to take priority. Those choices shut the people we care about most out of our lives. Stressing our ambitions rather than our friendships makes vulnerability impossible. And being vulnerable is a key ingredient in healthy relationships.

People who have experienced emotional or physical trauma often put *others* first in their lives in an unhealthy way. Psychologists call this being co-dependent with another person. We struggle with making decisions when we are co-dependent because we wonder what our partner thinks. We don't understand how we feel apart from our partner's emotions. We experience low self-esteem and value the approval of others more than our opinion of ourselves, let alone God's.

Believers who wrestle with co-dependency struggle to navigate life in the shadowlands. They fear abandonment, find it hard to trust others, and do more than their share of the work to prove their worth. It is easy to fall into loving ourselves less.

When *God* is first in our lives, we connect to others in healthy ways. Instead of fearing closeness, or looking for too much intimacy, we depend on God to meet our needs. When we prioritize time with God, we fill up on His love and hope. When we fill up first, we have cared for ourselves, and we have something to offer others.

Losing a loved one exposes unhealthy ways we may have related to others in the past. We discover we were either too self-sufficient or too co-dependent. As we walk with Jesus in our grief journey, He reveals which unhealthy way of "doing life together" we struggled with the most. When we are aware our friendships are out of balance, we can look to Him to help us have right relationships.

Jesus often uses a Christian counselor or pastor to help us learn new ways of living based on God's truth.

Live It Out: When you notice you're out of balance in your relationships, go back to the greatest commandment and remember what Jesus said: God first, then others the way you love yourself. When you find unhealthy habits in your life, I suggest you write them down in the back of your Bible. Then, record scriptures that combat the lie you have believed in the past with the truth you know today. I recommend this practice to you because it has been helpful for me.

Thinking About Heaven

One of the ways Jesus gives us hope and healing on our grief journey is by correcting our wrong thinking about heaven. The apostle John describes the new heaven and new earth this way:

Then I saw a new heaven and a new earth; for the first heaven and the first earth passed away, and there is no longer any sea. And I saw the Holy City, new Jerusalem, coming down out of heaven from God, prepared as a bride adorned for her husband. And I heard a loud voice from the throne, saying, "Behold, the tabernacle of God is among the people, and He will dwell among them, and they shall be His people, and God Himself will be among them, and He will wipe away every tear from their eyes; and there will no longer be any death; there will no longer be any mourning, or crying, or pain; the first things have passed away."

Revelation 21:1-4 (NASB)

The shadowlands had blinded us to the light of the Holy City, but Jesus has taken the scales off our eyes. We thought we would always be emotionally lame and waiting without hope by the healing pool, but Jesus has shown us the river that makes glad the city of God. Like orphans, we had hesitated to believe that we could ever sit at God's table, but Jesus has prepared a place for us more beautiful and wonderful than our tear-soaked eyes can believe.

Yes, we are walking through the shadowlands, but heaven will be better than the best times on earth. Nothing will separate us from God's love. Life-changing conversations with old and new friends will never be cut short. No sickness. No accidents. No murders. No wars. No suffering. No sorrow. No death.

Holli's death didn't ruin the plans God has made for our lives. Now I know the activities we didn't do together here are just empty shadows of what we will do together there. We will enjoy a cabin nestled among majestic mountains. We will travel the universe exploring God's breathtaking creation. We will experience no language barrier with believers from other countries and see how every culture makes heaven even more gorgeous and glorious. Every plan God gave us that I thought would happen here will happen in the best place it could—heaven.

Everything I loved and looked forward to in the shadowlands will find its final fulfillment in heaven. Mountains and valleys, rivers and snowfall, flowers and trees, lions and lambs, swords and plowshares—God will transform them into what they were meant to be. Music. Dancing. Laughing. Embracing. Every nation and culture adds beauty and joy to the Heavenly City.

All the beauty and wonder of heaven are possible only because of Jesus' death on the cross. We will see all these things only if we have put our trust in Jesus as the Savior for our sins. Jesus said He is the *only* way to the Father and eternal life. He also said anyone who tries to enter heaven another way is a thief and a robber. The Father and Spirit would never consider letting a person into heaven apart from believing in the death, burial, and resurrection of the Son. To do so would dishonor Jesus and break the fellowship the three of them have enjoyed for eternity.

The fact Jesus is the only way to heaven creates hard questions, though. What if your loved one wasn't a believer? What if you're not sure you want to go to heaven if your loved one isn't there? How could a loving God send your loved one to a place of eternal torment? I certainly don't have all the answers but do have some thoughts to consider.

First, the life, death, and resurrection of Jesus shows us the character of God. The Father's heart is to bless and not curse, give life instead of death, and redeem instead of calling fire down on our heads. God is not willing that any should perish and that means He is working all the time to make sure none do. You can be confident that God was working in the heart of your loved one all their life to bring them to Him.

Second, God's thoughts and ways are a million times higher than our own. We picture earthly judges and courtrooms when we think about the final judgment. Thinking that God's judgment will be the same as ours is like looking at a pebble and saying you understand all the mountains of the world. You can be confident God's judgment will take every aspect of your loved one's experience into account, not just whether they said the sinner's prayer or not.

Third, Jesus clearly taught that many people who think they are going to heaven will not be there, and others who people think won't make it ... will. How can that be? God doesn't judge by the outward appearance but the heart of a person. We can't judge another person's words or actions, only God can. You have no idea the talks your loved one had with God, even though they may have told you they didn't believe. You have no idea what their last words were to God, even if they were killed in a tragic accident. You can be confident that you didn't fully know the heart of your loved one and their most secret thoughts—only God did.

I am not saying everyone will go to heaven despite what they decide about Jesus as Savior. What I am saying is we don't have enough information on this side of heaven to make a judgment call. No one can be sure of another person's eternal dwelling place. But we can be sure of our own. And if your loved one made it to heaven (despite your concerns they did not), they certainly would not want your questions to block you from experiencing the abundant life Jesus died to give you.

Live It Out: Everything beautiful in this world is merely a shadow of something vastly better in heaven. Spend time thinking or journaling about the most beautiful landscapes you have seen in your life. Spend time thinking or journaling about the most precious acts of love you have experienced. When you have them clearly in your mind, ask the Lord to give you holy imagination to picture what those landscapes and acts look like in heaven. Thank Him for the shadows you have seen and the light you will see someday with your loved one in heaven.

Then Face-to-Face

Someday I will close my eyes and wake up in heaven, just like Holli did. I will see Jesus face-to-face. What a day of rejoicing that will be!

> *For now, we see in a mirror, dimly, but then face-to-face. Now I know in part, but then I shall know just as I also am known.*
>
> *I Corinthians 13:12 (NKJV)*

Jesus will answer all our questions. His love will fill our hearts, minds, souls, and bodies. Today, our view of heaven is dim because of sin and that's ok; we know our redemption draws close. Jesus will redeem all the brokenness, suffering, and injustices of our lives. He will restore everything damaged by sin and selfishness. He will put everything right. We will never suffer loss again.

Our loved ones have a unique perspective because they have already passed from this life to the next. They see families reunited in heaven every day. Hugging. Kissing. Eyes sparkling with joy. They know our time on earth seems long, but is just a breath, and we will join them soon.

When I think about what heaven will be like, I imagine Holli will take me to our family mansion and introduce me to our neighbors. She will giggle because our family and friends all live in one big neighborhood. Please visit! We would love to have you over for Sunday lunch—a tradition our family preserved even after Holli passed away. Maybe you will be there when St. Augustine or Mother Theresa are eating with us. Or perhaps you will be there when Billy Graham tells some of his best stories.

After we've eaten, I'll sit down at the keyboard and Holli will begin to sing a sweet song of worship to Jesus. Our oldest son will join in on the bass, our second son will take up his guitar, our youngest son will play the drums, and my daughter will join her mother in a beautiful duet. All my children's spouses will join in according to their gifts and dreams, and don't forget the grandchildren! They will dance with tambourines like Miriam at the Red Sea. Our little worship band will sing and play together again.

I look forward to having you in the worship band, too. If you've always wanted to learn how to play the guitar, rest assured you will play it in heaven. If you've always wanted to sing like an angel, you will in the Holy City. No choir on earth can touch how beautiful we will sound worshiping together in our cozy living room.

Better than all of that, we will talk and walk with Jesus. Some believers think we will spend eternity around His throne worshipping Him, but there will be so much more. Jesus will show us parts of heaven He knows we will enjoy. His loving, peaceful presence will be everywhere and light up the universe. No more unsettling doubts, sad holidays, or traumatic memories. Loneliness and depression will be gone—replaced by an eternal community filled with faith, hope, and love.

Live It Out: Spend time today meditating about God's plan throughout history. Think through His mighty works in the past. Think about believers in the past who have done great works in His name. Ponder testimonies of God's power working in the world you have heard recently.

Joshua commanded the children of Israel to build a memorial of twelve stones after they crossed the Jordan.

Create your own memorial to God and write down twelve truths you believe God wants you to remember from this book. Write one truth on each stone and carry one of the stones with you daily to remind you that God is working in your life.

▼ ▼ ▼ ▼ ▼

Our band of grieving, believing people is walking through the valley of grief with Jesus. You are not alone, and neither am I. God grant us eyes to see the light ahead and His light in each other. God grant us the grace and mercy to not shrink back but push forward, placing our grief and tears in His nail-scarred hands.

When Satan whispers his lies, remember these truths. It may help to ask yourself the question:

Jesus, what truth do I need to remember today?

Ground yourself on God's plan–His promise that heaven is coming, and Jesus is with us even in the shadowlands.

9

YOUR JOURNEY FORWARD

Losing a loved one changes our world forever. In the early months of our grief, we struggle with fears and tears while we try to make sense out of what happened. We ask "Why?" and feel betrayed by God—especially if we had a close relationship with Him before our spouse died. Our bodies respond to the trauma in ways that make it hard to resume a normal life.

Most of us don't know how to grieve well, so we can spend years in an endless cycle of sorrow and suffering. We start to believe that nothing will ever change, and we will always live in a bad place. I found myself thinking those hopeless thoughts after my wife died. You may be living in that empty house on despair street yourself right now.

But you don't have to stay there, child of the Living God. You have learned skills in this book that will help you through your grief journey. You have started to build skills that will serve you well for the rest of your life. You have a toolbox of proven skills to overcome whatever loss life may throw your way. And the reality is most of us will suffer loss again - the loss of a job, or a friend, or our health.

The GROW plan gives you a map to follow as you walk through the valley of the shadow of death. Following the GROW plan does not guarantee your trip will be easier, but it does promise you will avoid many of the dead-ends where those who grieve often find themselves stuck. You will still need to go slow and remember some days it will be two steps forward, and one back. That's what my journey has looked like and the journeys of my GriefShare® friends.

So, how should you start your journey? Begin by spending time in prayer each morning asking God what His three GOALS are for you that day. As you master this skill, God will reveal ROADBLOCKS that are keeping you from moving forward. Ask Him to help you remove them by His power and not your own. Setting goals and removing roadblocks is only half of the journey, though. OWNING our weaknesses and failures with humility starts an avalanche of grace in our hearts. Finally, we realize that God has used our grief to deepen our WALK with Him and a richer walk with God lasts forever.

You have learned to ask four simple questions using the GROW plan:

- Holy God, what are the three things You want me to do today?

- Holy Father, is there a roadblock in my way that You and I need to work through?

- Holy Spirit, what do I need to own today?

- Holy Jesus, what truth do I need to remember today as I walk with you?

These questions will keep you moving forward, but you already know it won't be in a straight line. Grief work demands all our heart, mind, soul, and body. There is no greater trial you will meet in this life. And the days will come when you lie on the battlefield wounded and wondering if you can take another step.

What should you do when you feel stuck in grief? Return to the first question and start again. Don't give up but thank God that He is jealous for you. He has not left or deserted you, but you have another opportunity to practice your grief skills again. And on days when you thought you had finished the journey, but waves of grief come crashing in yet again, keep holding Jesus' hand. We find our God is on the mountaintop and in our misery all the same.

Sailors used to tie themselves to the masts during frightening storms so they would not be swept overboard by the violent surge of waves. Similarly, tie yourself to Jesus. He will show you the way forward. Jesus will give you a deep flourishing life you could never have believed before the death of your loved one. He will open your eyes to see what is real and what are lies the evil one is telling you. Nothing can take you out of the hands of Jesus. Tie yourself to Him and live again.

EPILOGUE

Knowing Holli made me a better person. So much of who I am today is because of her. She showed me how to be concerned for others, have a servant's heart, and be more like Jesus. Even our occasional conflicts made me grow as a husband, father, pastor, and missionary.

When Holli died, I thought death had won but now I know that it did not. God and I won. God promised He was guiding me along the *best* pathway for my life. I did not understand why Holli died and I still had many questions, but the day would come when He would reveal everything.

God existed long before death entered our world and is the God of the living. Holli is more alive and "real" today than she was on earth because of Jesus' resurrection. God is eternal. Death is a temporary a phase.

Because of Jesus' resurrection, my memories of Holli are only shadows of the joy I will experience with her one day. I will walk with her again in heaven and our relationship will pick up right where we left off here on earth. Even better, our time in heaven will be sweeter because of how Jesus is continuing to change me here on earth.

I've learned that just because I doubt doesn't mean something is not true. God always holds me; my job is to cast down thinking that exalts itself above Him. I've learned that Satan is both the Father of Lies and the Father of Death. So, that makes death a liar.

Practicing the GROW plan helped me work through my grief in a healthy way by experiencing Jesus more deeply. Setting small faith, hope, and love goals kept me moving toward the Heavenly City. Following Jesus with the GROW plan grounded me in God's resurrection power instead of death's crooked sway. Slowly I saw the roadblocks of doubt, depression, and discouragement shrink and become more manageable.

Using the GROW plan kept me from getting stuck in my sorrow. Jesus showed me how to own my anger, stop soul-defeating questions, and fight loneliness with His truth and not let it cripple me emotionally. I pray the GROW plan will do the same for you.

Believers throughout history have found the skills of the GROW plan a powerful way to walk through a loved one's death. These four simple steps renew us each day and move us from glory to glory. We begin to see more of God's glory and fewer of death's shadows. This simple plan gives perseverance and promise on the darkest day.

We don't leave our loved ones behind but carry them with us the rest of our days. Grief is not a problem we solve but a skill we learn. Sorrow and sadness whisper to us how much we loved, and others loved us in this life.

▼ ▼ ▼ ▼ ▼

Holli will be there waiting for me when I arrive in heaven. She sees us now. She hasn't held our grandson in the shadowlands, but she sees him from heaven with clear eyes and a full heart. We will see her again. Jesus' resurrection is too powerful for anything else to be true.

Holli sees how our family has joined the fellowship of suffering with Jesus because of her death. She also sees the fruit her death has produced in our lives. Great was our loss when she died, but greater our gain now from the glory of her life. Unless a seed falls to the ground, it can't grow and produce a harvest. Holli's death continues to move her loved ones from glory to glory.

In the process of sharing this journey of healing with you, I often heard Holli cheering me on, and I captured what I would imagine her saying to me. With her words, I conclude.

Dear sweetheart,

Congratulations on finishing the book. I know you didn't think you could complete it because it was so hard emotionally, but you did and I'm proud of you. Your vulnerability will help others know they are not alone in their journey. I always appreciated your transparency and am sure others will feel the same way as they read about your struggles.

Wow! I always knew you loved me, but I had no idea how much. Even though you were relational and good at communicating, I guess you were still a guy (wink, wink). Now that I see the record of your life, I realize the heavy emotional load you have carried inside for so many years. I can also see the times I wasn't there for you and I'm sorry. I can tell you, though, that Jesus was always there. He has never left your side.

Please don't be so hard on yourself, babe. I know you feel like you didn't describe heaven adequately in the book, but that is a journey each person must take themselves. I know you feel like the first two chapters were too emotionally raw, but they weren't. You are just a man who loves Jesus and wants to help people. Let that be all you seek. Let that be all you need.

I'm looking forward to seeing you and the kids again. It must seem like such a long time there, but it feels truly short here. I have some surprises for everyone when you arrive. You can't imagine what it's like to be in a place where the love of God permeates absolutely everything—from every relationship down to each blade of grass.

I have fond memories about how we made decisions together. You and I would imagine both of us sitting at a table and Jesus sitting on the other side. In the middle of the table were a piece of paper and a pen. We would take the pen and write "Yes" on the piece of paper. Then we would give it to Jesus. He would write what He wanted us to do and hand it back to us. We would stand and start the task Jesus had given to us.

What a wonderful way to live! I'm so thankful for how you always tried to lead us toward God. If I hadn't met you, sweetheart, I would have ended up a librarian somewhere. God filled our lives with so many adventures because we always said "Yes" to Him first. Thank you for the precious love we shared on earth together. Thank you for the excitement you brought into my life.

I know your journey has been so hard, babe. But it's time to come to the table again. It's time to write "Yes" on the paper and give it to Jesus. It's time to start off on the next adventure He has for you. Please say "Yes" and keep pressing forward ... for us and for Him.

I still love you to the moon and back,

Holli

ACKNOWLEDGMENTS

Ery author should have an outstanding editor and I am blessed with three: Adele Booysen, Tara Cooper, and Kim Goodrich. All of your insights made the final manuscript clearer and easier to understand. You also helped me push through the grief that revisited me while writing this book. Thank you.

The Union University community surrounded our family after Holli's death and helped us walk through dark days. Thank you to: Dr. Scott and Tamarin Huelin, Dr. George and Pat Guthrie, Drs. Hal and Mary Anne Poe, Dr. Brad and Diane Green, Mrs. Haelim Allen, Bart and Audra Teague, Dr. David Thomas, Dr. Nathan and Leah Finn, John and Cathy Windham, Dr. John and Tina Netland, Melanie Edwards, Allie Curry, and Matthew Marshall.

One of the blessings of being a missionary is all the friends God sends to help you on your mission. The list below are friends who ministered to our family in significant ways during our grief journey: Beth Avery, Kim Barr, Dale and Anita Beyer, Tim and Karen Bickers, Lisa Blair, John and Jayla Briscoe, Debbie Childress, Rev. Will

Chenault, Julianne Clark, Dave and Tricia Coburn, Don Cramer, Rev. Kevin and Wendi Cude, Vicki Cummings, Gilbert and Ruby David, Nancy Donahoo, Gene Ennis, Dr. Scott Ericson, LaMont and Jackie Ford, Dr. John and Nancy Freeman, Rob and Donna Freshour, Craig and Kara Garrison, Hal and Annamarie Hamilton, Donald and Debbie Hintze, Alex and Joretta Hutton, Cody and Sharaya Isaacson, Duane and Suzanne Jones, Raymond and Della Jones, Rev. Vann and Norma Kissel, George and Kay Luker, Jenni McClung, Diane Matheny, Chuck Maxwell, Andrew and Jennifer Miller, Gary and Johni Morgan, Keith Owens, Dr. Ricky and Jane Paris, Amy Ragon, Carla Richardson, Michelle Ridinger, Cynthia Santana, Paul and Riley Sigler, Rhonda Sigler, Jackie Signaigo, Dr. Ray and Stephanie Smith, Dr. Ned and Wanda Stewart, Raelen VanDuzer, Rev. Brian Viera, Gary and Carolyn Watkins, and Rev. Dan Wooldridge.

My mother, Glenna Iwami, stood with me through some of the toughest points of my grief journey. Thank you for being a safe harbor in the storm.

I would also like to thank Holli's family for their love and support through the years: Dr. Roy (deceased) and Jean Fish, Steve and Marci Fish, Dr. Jeff and Holly Fish, and Drs. Charles and Jenni Pastoor.

Finally, special thanks to my grown children, their spouses, and my first grandson: Jeffrey and Linnea Lancaster with Rhys, Zachary and Bethany Lancaster, Jeremiah and Karis Murila, and Zane Lancaster. You have always been and will always be mom and my greatest delights. I have no doubt that she is proud of the men and women you have become.

THANK YOU

Before you go, I'd like to say "thank you" again for purchasing my book and I hope you have been blessed by it. I know you could have picked from dozens of books, but you felt the Lord leading you to mine.

Again, a big thank you for buying *Death Is A Liar* and reading it to the end.

Could I ask a *small* favor? Please take a minute to leave a review for this book at go.lightkeeperbooks.com/e-dil-rev.

Think of your brief review as giving a short testimony that helps others know if this book is what they need to grow in their spiritual life.

Your review will encourage me to continue to write books that help people grow in their walk with Jesus. And if you loved it, please let me know that too! :)

BONUS

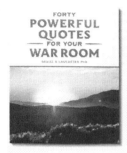

Don't forget to download your free *Powerful Prayers Bonus Pak*! The free Pak includes three resources to help you pray powerful prayers:

- •100 Promises – Audio Version
- •40 Faith-Building Quotes
- •40 Powerful Prayers.

All are suitable for framing. Download your free *Powerful Prayers Bonus Pak* at go.lightkeeperbooks.com/powerpak

I've also included an excerpt from my bestselling book *Fear is a Liar*. God has blessed many through this book and I wanted to give you a chance to "try before you buy." To order *Fear is a Liar*, visit go.lightkeeperbooks.com/e-fil

FEAR IS A LIAR

HOW TO STOP ANXIOUS THOUGHTS AND EXPERIENCE GOD'S LOVE

DANIEL B LANCASTER PhD

INTRODUCTION

This is a simple book about how to overcome your fears and experience God's love more deeply.

Doesn't it seem like people used to live simpler, happier lives? Now, many of us are slowly turning into fearful, suspicious people. And fearful, suspicious people are often lonely people. We worry about being rejected by our friends, our loved ones dying, losing our jobs, and failing as parents. We worry about sexual predators, increased crime, the rise in severe weather events, and whether we will have enough money when we retire.

When you try to stop thinking about your fears, they only get stronger. Then, you try to ignore your fears, but that makes them bigger. What's a person to do?

As a missionary, I've faced all kinds of terrifying situations.

I've been in earthquakes and hotel fires. I've been trailed by the secret police. Our family moved to a place where soldiers with machine-guns guarded every major intersection in the capital city. (You can imagine how terrifying it was just driving around.) I also know firsthand about the fears that come when ovarian cancer takes your precious wife of thirty years.

I remember a time overseas when all the blood in my body settled in my legs. My wife and I had just learned a mother cobra and her babies decided to live in the flower bed where our children loved to play. A friend discovered the four-foot cobra when it raised its head and began to sway back and forth. Thankfully, he killed the venomous snake and her offspring while we were out of the country renewing our visas. I'll never forget how white my wife's face looked when she heard the news and how I held her arm to steady her.

Our family faced many fearful experiences while we ministered in a foreign land. We had to learn how to deal with our fears or be overwhelmed by them. Sometimes we failed miserably in our fight against fear. Slowly though, we learned the steps in the **LOVE Plan** and saw more victories than defeats. I believe that God will help you do the same.

Jesus said in the last days that fear would increase on the earth. Clearly, people struggle with worry and anxiety today more than ever.

And there will be signs in sun and moon and stars, and on the earth distress of nations in perplexity because of the roaring of the sea and the waves, people fainting with fear and with foreboding of what is coming on the world. For the powers of the heavens will be shaken.

Luke 21:25-26

In this book, you will learn a biblical plan to overcome whatever fear you may face. God hasn't given you a spirit of fear and wants you to defeat the flaming lying arrows of the Evil One.

You will benefit along the way by developing a deeper walk with God and love for other people. You will also discover some good ways to do self-care. This book will teach you how to fill your love tank and not run on "almost empty" any longer.

This book will teach you how to:

- Identify your root fears
- Understand why fears are so powerful
- Learn how Jesus dealt with fear
- Practice a 4-step biblical plan to stop fear in its tracks
- Experience deeper love for God, others, and yourself

At the end of this book, my prayer is that you will be able to say:

> *I prayed to the Lord, and he answered me. He freed me from all my fears.*
>
> *Psalm 34:4*

Always remember, friend, fear is a liar. I've shared the truth of these principles throughout the world, and they have helped many overcome their fears. I believe God is going to do the same in your life. As you practice the *LOVE Plan*, you will hear the Holy Spirit more clearly, and your fears will lose their power over your mind, heart, soul, and spirit.

And it gets even better: You will be able to share these simple truths with your friends and family and see their lives transformed as well. Just imagine the gift you will give your children of knowing how to let perfect love cast out their fears.

As we journey through this book together, you will learn a new way of living, conquer your fears, and become more like Jesus. God wants that. You want that. I want that. So, let's get started.

In the next chapter, we'll travel back to the first recorded fear in the Bible.

1

WHY WE WORRY

Worry often gives a small thing a big shadow.
— SWEDISH PROVERB

Fears are tricky, little devils. They are like the little weeds in your yard or garden—you hardly give them a thought. But, the longer you wait to remove them, the more weeds they produce. If you wait too long, they choke out the good plants and everything looks ...well ... just ugly.

When you feel like the whole world is ugly, it is a sign you have a fear problem. When your relationships feel ugly, it is a sign you have a fear problem. When your God-ordained future seems ugly, it is a sign you have a fear problem.

The first step in overcoming fears is to understand why and where they originally entered the world. That's what we will explore in this chapter. I will show you how Satan first enslaved humanity with fear. It turns out fear and worry have filled people's hearts and minds for an awfully long time.

Along the way, you will discover how the Hater tries to manipulate your mind and heart. You will learn how the Hater tries to turn the good from God in your life into evil. You will realize the Hater wants you to over analyze everything in your life and paralyze you with fear. This gives Satan even more time to fill your mind with untruths.

Just being aware of his evil schemes will help you walk on the narrow Path of Love instead of wandering on the broad Path of Fear. Understanding why you have fears is an important step to becoming more confident as you fight them.

My prayer is you will once again see the beauty of God brighten every corner of your life. To do that, we will go back to a garden called Eden.

THE NARROW PATH OF LOVE

Imagine working and playing in the Garden of Eden before Adam and Eve sinned. Everything they did had so much meaning.

Adam and Eve looked forward to the cool of the day. God would come down and they shared their hearts with Him. He shared His heart with them too. It's not hard to imagine what their conversations were like. Love. Love. Love.

Eve shared with God how proud she was of Adam. He was so smart; he had named all the animals! Adam smiled sheepishly and said it was nothing. Eve made him feel ten-feet tall.

Adam shared with Eve how lonely life was before she came. Adam thanked God every evening for giving him such an incredible gift. Eve probably blushed and told Adam to stop making such a big deal out of her.

God praised Adam for his heart to be a rock for Eve and someone she could always count on. They noticed a tear in God's eye when He praised Adam for sacrificing for his wife.

God praised Eve for how beautiful she was making everything in the garden and for her creativity. Eve felt so honored and cherished and celebrated.

Oh, the joy to walk on the Path of Love with no fear!

Adam and Eve probably talked with God about having children. They had seen the animals give birth and wondered if humans could too. Or would God make their children like He had made them? Eve looked forward to a happy family that would make the world an even better place.

Adam asked God what had caused him to feel different inside when he climbed too high in a tree.

God explained He had put an emotion in Adam and Eve that told them when they were in danger. He had given them this feeling because He loved them and wanted them to be safe.

Just being close to God filled them with love and confidence. Walking with Him made them feel incredibly strong and wise. God answered every question about their world.

They laughed. They dreamed. They couldn't wait until tomorrow.

THE BROAD PATH OF FEAR

But everything changed one day. Adam and Eve stopped walking on the narrow Path of Love. Genesis 3 tells about the painful entry of sin and fear into our world.

> *Now the serpent was more cunning than any beast of the field which the Lord God had made. And he said to the woman, "Has God indeed said, 'You shall not eat of every tree of the garden'?"*
>
> *Genesis 3:1 (NKJV)*

Satan lures Eve down the Path of Fear by questioning God's command. The Great Manipulator, Satan, takes something good that God has said and makes it sound wrong or petty. He fills her mind with lies.

If you have ever known a self-centered person, you know the drill. Start by getting your target to recosider a small action or decision. Cause them to doubt their own instincts and to trust that you have their best interests in mind. But it's all a scam. You're luring them into your trap. This is exactly what Satan did in the garden.

Now Eve has started down the Path of Fear, thinking Satan's thoughts, and she doesn't even realize it. Satan has already deceived a third of the angels of heaven into following him. Eve has zero experience dealing with manipulation and deception. There's no way she's going to win.

> *And the woman said to the serpent, "We may eat the fruit of the trees of the garden; but of the fruit of the tree which is in the midst of the garden, God has said, 'You shall not eat it, nor shall you touch it, lest you die.'"*
>
> *Genesis 3:2-3 (NKJV)*

Getting into a conversation with Satan is never a good idea, but that's exactly what Eve did. Satan is the Father of Lies and doesn't play fair. Even though Eve simply tells Satan what God commanded, she is still speaking with the Enemy of her soul. Even Michael, the archangel, knew better than talk to Satan without God's help (Jude 9).

> *Then the serpent said to the woman, "You will not surely die. For God knows that in the day you eat of it your eyes will be opened, and you will be like God, knowing good and evil."*
>
> *Genesis 3:4-5 (NKJV)*

Now that Eve is thinking the way Satan wants her to, he openly questions God's goodness. Satan wants Eve to believe that God doesn't have her best interest in mind. God created Eve as a helpmeet; her deep desire is to work with Adam to create a beautiful world.

Meanwhile, Satan tells her that she is missing out. God is holding out on her and her husband. She wonders if God hasn't been telling the whole truth when she and Adam talked with Him in the cool of the day. Was God hiding something? Maybe He hasn't been meeting her needs as well as she thought He was. Satan has kindled a fire of suspicion in her mind and heart. Can God, in fact, be trusted?

> *So when the woman saw that the tree was good for food, that it was pleasant to the eyes, and a tree desirable to make one wise, she took of its fruit and ate. She also gave to her husband with her, and he ate.*
>
> *Genesis 3:6 (NKJV)*

Eve relies on her own judgment instead of God's Will and God's Word. The fruit looked good. The fruit looked beautiful. The fruit made one wise like God. It's all good.

She takes a bite of the fruit and nothing happens immediately. So, she gives it to Adam. She probably felt like she had made the best decision in the world, and to show her husband how much she loved him, she shared it with him. Just think how they could help their kids if they were wise like God!

> Then the eyes of both of them were opened, and they knew that they were naked; and they sewed fig leaves together and made themselves coverings.
>
> Genesis 3:7 (NKJV)

Enter the first fear: shame. Disobedience opened their eyes and closed their hearts. Adam and Eve saw their nakedness and felt shame. They responded by sewing fig leaves together, trying to hide their shame.

Satan knew the more shame Adam and Eve felt, the more fears they would believe. They soon found that one feeling of unworthiness in the heart can easily create ten fears in the mind.

It's not hard to imagine Eve crying and apologizing to Adam for what had happened. Her wrong thinking had created overwhelming suffering for her and her husband. Eve thought she was doing something good.

But everything changed to bad ... extremely bad.

Download *Fear is a Liar* at go.lightkeeperbooks.com/e-fil

CHRISTIAN SELF-HELP

Available on

Overcome fear, shame, and other spiritual attacks
that hold you back from being all God created you to be.

Visit go.lightkeeperbooks.com/selfhelp to learn more

Coming Soon

SATAN IS A LIAR
Satan only cares about himself and stopping you.
Learn how to overcome the greatest narcissist of all time.

Lightkeeper Kids Series

"Very sweet! Easy for kids to understand and relate to!"

Visit go.lightkeeperbooks.com/lkk
to learn more

ABOUT THE AUTHOR

Daniel B. Lancaster (PhD) enjoys training others to become passionate followers of Christ. He has planted two churches in America and trained over 5,000 people in Southeast Asia as a strategy coordinator with the International Mission Board. He served as Assistant Vice-President for University Ministries at Union University and currently is the Director of Coaching at Cornerstone International. He has four grown children and a delightful grandson.

Dr. Dan is available for speaking and training events. Contact him at dan@lightkeeperbooks.com to arrange a meeting for your group.

Made in United States
Orlando, FL
21 September 2023

37145691R00085